T0285399

WALKING IN THE PICOS DE EUROPA

42 WALKS AND TREKS IN SPAIN'S FIRST NATIONAL PARK

by Robin Walker

JUNIPER HOUSE, MURLEY MOSS,
OXENHOLME ROAD, KENDAL, CUMBRIA LA9 7RL
www.cicerone.co.uk

© Robin Walker 2023
Second edition 2023
ISBN: 978 1 85284 536 0
First edition 1989

Printed in China on responsibly sourced paper on behalf of Latitude Press Ltd
A catalogue record for this book is available from the British Library.
All photographs are by the author.

Route mapping by Lovell Johns www.lovelljohns.com
Contains OpenStreetMap.org data © OpenStreetMap
contributors, CC-BY-SA. NASA relief data courtesy of ESRI

Dedication
To friendships new and renewed. To friends who went on ahead.

Updates to this guide

While every effort is made by our authors to ensure the accuracy of guide-books as they go to print, changes can occur during the lifetime of an edition. Any updates that we know of for this guide will be on the Cicerone website (www.cicerone.co.uk/536/updates), so please check before planning your trip. We also advise that you check information about such things as transport, accommodation and shops locally. Even rights of way can be altered over time. We are always grateful for information about any discrepancies between a guidebook and the facts on the ground, sent by email to updates@cicerone.co.uk or by post to Cicerone, Juniper House, Murley Moss, Oxenholme Road, Kendal, LA9 7RL.

Register your book: To sign up to receive free updates, special offers and GPX files where available, register your book in your Cicerone library at www.cicerone.co.uk.

Front cover: Setting off up the Duje Valley (Walk 17)

CONTENTS

Map key 7
Route summary table 8
Preface 13

INTRODUCTION 17
Location and geography 18
Geology 18
Climate and weather 19
Plants and flowers 20
Wildlife 22
The National Park 24
Getting there 26
Getting around 26
Language and money 27
Where to stay 28
When to visit 28
What to take 30
Maps 30
GPS in the Picos 31
Roads, tracks and paths 32
Safety 34
Emergencies 34
Using this guide 34

CANGAS DE ONÍS 37
Walk 1   La Cruz de Priena 41
Walk 2   La Majada de Belbín 46
Walk 3   La Buferrera and Los Lagos 52
Walk 4   Covadonga from Los Lagos 57
Walk 5   Ario and El Jultayu 62
Walk 6   El Mirador de Ordiales 68
Walk 7   Tour of the Torre de Santa María 73
Walk 8   Torre les Travieses 76
Walk 9   La Jocica and La Senda del Arcediano 79

CABRALES 85
Walk 10   Pueblos de Cabrales 88
Walk 11   Cabeza de Juanrobre. 93
Walk 12   El Cuetón 96
Walk 13   Monte Camba 103
Walk 14   Vao los Llobos. 107
Walk 15   Pico de San Carlos 112
Walk 16   Pica el Jierru 116
Walk 17   Colláu Cambureru. 120
Walk 18   Cabrones and Urriellu. 126

LIÉBANA 133
Walk 19   Pueblos de Liébana. 136
Walk 20   Pico Jano. 141
Walk 21   Vega de Liordes. 145
Walk 22   Alto la Padierna. 149
Walk 23   El Cable and La Jenduda 154
Walk 24   Peña Vieja 158
Walk 25   Los Puertos de Áliva 163
Walk 26   Peña Oviedo. 167

VALDEÓN 171
Walk 27   Pico Cebolleda 174
Walk 28   La Torre Salinas 178
Walk 29   Collado Jermoso 182
Walk 30   El Valle del Arenal. 186
Walk 31   Pueblos de Valdeón. 190
Walk 32   La Travesona 194
Walk 33   The Cares Gorge 199

SAJAMBRE 205
Walk 34   Pica Beza 207
Walk 35   Vega Huerta 211
Walk 36   Pico Jario 216
Walk 37   Pueblos de Sajambre. 220
Walk 38   Sajambre es Bosque 224

TREKKING 231
Trek 1   Tour of the Western Massif 232
Trek 2   Tour of the Central Massif 235

Trek 3   Tour of the Eastern Massif 238
Trek 4   Ruta de la Reconquista – GR 202 241

Appendix A   Useful contacts and website addresses 245
Appendix B   Glossary 247
Appendix C   Huts of the Picos de Europa 250

Acknowledgments

First and foremost, my heartfelt thanks to Ann, Gus and Terry. The time we spent together in 2018 and 2019 was fundamental to the development of the guidebook. Thanks also to Sue, John, Andrew, Rebecca, Bob, Eric, Alberto, Germán, Consuelo, Alba and Isabel for their generous company on different walks. Lastly, my thanks to Juanjo Álvarez, of Casa Cipriano, Sotres, for his suggestions prior to my beginning the field work.

A storm brewing over the Central Massif

Mountain safety

Every mountain walk has its dangers, and those described in this guidebook are no exception. All who walk or climb in the mountains should recognise this and take responsibility for themselves and their companions along the way. The author and publisher have made every effort to ensure that the information contained in this guide was correct when it went to press, but, except for any liability that cannot be excluded by law, they cannot accept responsibility for any loss, injury or inconvenience sustained by any person using this book.

International distress signal *(emergency only)*
Six blasts on a whistle (and flashes with a torch after dark) spaced evenly for one minute, followed by a minute's pause. Repeat until an answer is received. The response is three signals per minute followed by a minute's pause.

Helicopter rescue
The following signals are used to communicate with a helicopter:

Help needed: raise both arms above head to form a 'Y'

Help not needed: raise one arm above head, extend other arm downward

Stand with your back to the wind when signaling so as to indicate wind direction to the helicopter pilot.

Emergency telephone numbers
If telephoning from the UK the dialling code is:
Spain: 0034
To call out the Mountain Rescue, ring 112, the international emergency number.

Weather reports
Go to the AEMET (Spanish State Meteorological Agency) – https://www.aemet. es/en/eltiempo/prediccion/montana. Click on the Picos de Europa for a detailed four-day forecast in Spanish.

Mountain rescue can be very expensive – be adequately insured.

Symbols used on route maps

~	route	*	viewpoint
~ ~ ~	alternative route	▲	cave
•••	tunnel on route	⊙	rest/picnic area
Ⓢ	start point	🅿	parking
Ⓕ	finish point	⊞	cemetery
ⓈⒻ	start/finish point	⊕	cable car station
❯	route direction	•	water feature
	woodland	•	other feature
	urban areas		
■ 🚌	station/funicular		
⛟	cable car		
■	bus stop		
▲	peak		
⬆	manned refuge/hut		
⬆	unmanned refuge		
■	building		
☦	church		
≍	pass		
=	bridge		

Relief
in metres

2600–2800
2400–2600
2200–2400
2000–2200
1800–2000
1600–1800
1400–1600
1200–1400
1000–1200
800–1000
600–800
400–600
200–400
0–200

SCALE: 1:50,000

0 kilometres	0.5		1
0 miles		0.5	

Contour lines are drawn at 25m intervals
and highlighted at 100m intervals.

Walk maps are at 1:150,000 unless otherwise indicated (see scale bar).

GPX files for all routes can be downloaded free at www.cicerone.co.uk/536/GPX.

ROUTE SUMMARY TABLE

Walk	Name	Start/Finish	Distance	Ascent/Descent	Grade	Time	Page
Cangas de Onís							
1	La Cruz de Priena	Castañeu de Corao	18km	890m	Difficult	6–7hr	41
2	La Majada de Belbín	Demués	22km	1200m	Difficult	8–9hr	46
3	La Buferrera and Los Lagos	Buferrera car park	5.9km	200m	Easy	3hr	52
4	Covadonga from Los Lagos	Buferrera car park/ Covadonga	10.5km	280m/1065m	Moderate	3–4hr	57
5	Ario and El Jultayu	Buferrera car park	19.6km	1275m	Very difficult	7–9hr	62
6	El Mirador de Ordiales	Buferrera car park	23.6km	1135m	Difficult	7–8hr	68
7	Tour of the Torre de Santa María	Vegarredonda	10.1km	1105m	Very difficult	4–5hr	73
8	Torre les Traviese	Vegarredonda	10.9km	1010m	Very difficult	4–5hr	76
9	La Jocica and La Senda del Arcediano	Collado de Angón	22	1120m	Difficult	7–8hr	79
Cabrales							
10	Pueblos de Cabrales	Ortigueru/Carreña	10.7km	345m/575m	Moderate	4hr	88

Walk	Name	Start/Finish	Distance	Ascent/Descent	Grade	Time	Page
11	Cabeza de Juanrobre	Arenas de Cabrales	11.4km	800m	Moderate	5–6hr	93
12	El Cuetón	Arenas de Cabrales/Poncebos	18.4km	1540m/1475m	Very difficult	8–10hr	96
13	Monte Camba	Tielve	13.5km	750m	Moderate	5–6hr	103
14	Vao los Llobos	Joyu el Teju	15.5km	700m	Moderate	5–6hr	107
15	Pico de San Carlos	Joyu el Teju	15.2km	1080m	Difficult	7–8hr	112
16	Pica el Jierru	Joyu el Teju	18.1km	1190m	Very difficult	7–9hr	116
17	Colláu Cambureru	Los Invernales del Texu	14.5km	1300m	Very difficult	7–9hr	120
18	Cabrones and Urriellu	Bulnes	16.1km	1800m	Very difficult	2 days	126
Liébana							
19	Pueblos de Liébana	Tama	13.5km	630m	Moderate	5–6hr	136
20	Pico Jano	Dobarganes	9.2km	600m	Moderate	4–5hr	141
21	Vega de Liordes	Fuente Dé	13.2km	1080m	Difficult	6–7h	145
22	Alto la Padierna	Fuente Dé	16.7km	1410m	Very difficult	7–9hr	149
23	El Cable and La Jenduda	Fuente Dé	9.7km	920m	Very difficult	5–6hr	154

Walk	Name	Start/Finish	Distance	Ascent/Descent	Grade	Time	Page
24	Peña Vieja	El Cable (upper station)	11.8km	1110m	Difficult	6–7hr	158
25	Los Puertos de Áliva	El Cable/Fuente Dé	13.9km	280m/1070m	Moderate	4–5hr	163
26	Peña Oviedo	Mogrovejo	10.8km	720m	Moderate	4hr	167
Valdeón							
27	Pico Cebolleda	Puerto de Panderruedas	13km	770m	Difficult	5–6hr	174
28	La Torre Salinas	Horcada de Valcavao	8.6km	820m	Difficult	5hr	178
29	Collado Jermoso	Cordiñanes	14.3km	1765m	Very difficult	8–10hr	182
30	El Valle del Arenal	Prada de Valdeón	12.6km	825m	Moderate	4–5hr	186
31	Pueblos de Valdeón	Posada de Valdeón	7.8km	360m	Easy	3hr	190
32	La Travesona	Posada de Valdeón	15km	1230m	Very difficult	7–9hr	194
33	The Cares Gorge	Posada de Valdeón/Poncebos	20km	160m/900m	Moderate	5–7hr	199
Sajambre							
34	Pica Beza	Soto de Sajambre	13.9km	1130m	Difficult	6–8hr	207
35	Vega Huerta	Vegabaño	16.6km	960m	Difficult	7–8hr	211

Walk	Name	Start/Finish	Distance	Ascent/Descent	Grade	Time	Page
36	Pico Jario	Vegabaño	10.9km	750m	Moderate	5hr	216
37	Pueblos de Sajambre	Oseja de Sajambre	11km	500m	Moderate	4hr	220
38	Sajambre es Bosque	Oseja de Sajambre	23.9km	1465m	Very difficult	9–11hr	224

Trekking

Walk	Name	Start/Finish	Distance	Ascent/Descent	Grade	Time	Page
Trek 1	Tour of the Western Massif	Posada de Valdeón	56.5km	3570m	Difficult	4 days	232
Trek 2	Tour of the Central Massif	Poncebos	63km	3055m	Moderate	4 days	235
Trek 3	Tour of the Eastern Massif	Mogrovejo/Potes	41.9km	2460m/2815m	Moderate	3 days	238
Trek 4	Ruta de la Reconquista – GR 202	Covadonga/Cosgaya	70.3km	4395m/3945m	Difficult	4 days	241

The tunnels on the Cares Gorge just below Caín (Walk 33)

PREFACE

Dawn from the Mirador Pedro Udaondo (Walk 10)

When I first visited Spain in the summer of 1979, my friends arranged for a local mountaineer to take me to the Picos de Europa. The journey was such an adventure that when we finally got to Poncebos, setting off to walk came as a relief. My relief was short-lived. Almost immediately our path was hanging off near vertical walls above a raging torrent. But anxiety turned to amazement when the gorge opened out and we entered Bulnes, a village without a road, a space without a time.

On leaving Bulnes the path entered a dank cleft, which we laboured up within the very guts of the mountain to reach the ruins of the shepherds' cabins at the Majada de Cambureru. By now, I was harbouring serious doubts about the day, but what I saw next dispelled every last one of them. Towering above me, glorious in the afternoon sun, was the west face of El Naranjo de Bulnes. I was speechless. How was it I had no idea of its existence? How was it that I knew nothing of these inspiring, rugged mountains? What other similar surprises lay in wait for me in the Picos?

The answer to my first two questions is the same now as it was then. For many mountaineers, the Pyrenees steal the limelight and relegate the Picos de Europa to a minor place. In 1979 this was in part because so little had been written about the Picos in English, and even in Spanish reliable information was hard come by.

As to my third question, endless surprises lay in wait for me, and a great many of them came together in my 1989 Cicerone guidebook. The emphasis of that first guide was on climbing – it was the outcome of me spending all my free time scaling the walls and towers of the three Picos massifs. More recently, walking has come to the fore in my life, and is the sole focus of this new guide.

All through the 1980s and 90s, walking was the penance that took me to the foot of a climb. Today, I relish a day's walking in the Picos de Europa. Back then, nothing below 1500m held any real value for me. Now I delight in walks at any altitude, and in all terrain. The joy comes in part from the benefits of walking as an activity. But it also comes from my discovery of a world of plants, birds and animals that I was so often blind to when climbing. A third of all Spanish vertebrates can be found in the Picos de Europa, for example, and thanks to the richness of the hay meadows and middle-mountain pastures, the same is true for more than 60% of the country's butterflies. Inventories of vascular plants in the Picos reach a staggering 1750 species, of which 157 are endemic. The vegetation in the range represents both the Atlantic and Mediterranean climates, which regularly lie cheek by jowl because of the effects of orientation, altitude and soil type. Centuries of human activity have modelled the landscape through a range of practices, some of which, like shepherding, are ancient and indisputably sustainable. Others, particularly mining, have been glaringly destructive and, whilst not to be welcomed back, they prove fascinating to explore as examples of industrial archaeology.

These and many more were among the surprises that lay in wait for me back in 1979. These and many more are among the surprises lie in wait for you now, just as they do for anyone curious enough to venture away from the more obvious draw of the Alps or the Pyrenees, and adventurous enough to walk among the cliffs and clefts that house the magic of these magnificent mountains.

The upper Dobra valley near Carombo (Walk 9)

The gullies and ridges of the Torre Friero from the Traviesa del Congosto (Walk 29)

INTRODUCTION

Looking towards Fuente Dé with the Tornos de Liordes track visible centre right (Walk 20)

The Pyrenees, the Sierra Nevada, the Guadarrama to the north of Madrid... the list of mountain ranges in Spain is as extensive as the country itself. But in the minds of many, the Picos de Europa are the jewel in the Spanish crown. This tiny gem, only 30km by 25km in size, climbs to over 2500m in numerous places, but plunges to below 100m in others, offering, as a result, walking for all tastes. From gentle strolls along fertile valley bottoms, to treks along gorges that slice through towering walls and peaks, to exacting high-mountain adventures over dry, cratered limestone, the variety of walks in the Picos de Europa means that there is something here for everyone.

Barely 20km south of the sea and 20km north of the plains of Castille, the Picos witness the intriguing effects of the Atlantic and Mediterranean climates rubbing up one against the other. Apparently exclusive habitats happily survive in close proximity, with north-facing slopes swathed in mature beech forest directly opposite rugged hillsides of thick Mediterranean scrub. This unique binomial makes the Picos a paradise for botanists and birdwatchers alike, but also gives rise to centuries-old rural practices that are still carried out today, and that are the justification for the National Park status the Picos de Europa now enjoy. Add to the equation the first-rate options for accommodation, the rich and varied cuisine, the favourable northern Spanish climate, plus the chance to mix demanding mountain days with long afternoons lazing on the beach, and you have all of the ingredients for an unforgettable holiday.

LOCATION AND GEOGRAPHY

The Picos de Europa straddle the autonomous regions of Asturias, Cantabria and Castilla y León in Northwest Spain. Although geologically they are part of the Cordillera Cantábrica, their unique character makes them a separate range in the minds of many mountaineers. The limits of the Picos de Europa are marked out to the east and west by the spectacular gorges of the rivers Deva and Sella, respectively, whilst the range itself is split into three distinct massifs by the north–south course of the rivers Duje and Cares. The three massifs are known quite simply as the Macizo Oriental (Eastern), the Macizo Central and the Macizo Occidental (Western). In addition, each massif has a historical name, these being, from east to west, de Ándara, de Los Urrieles and del Cornión.

GEOLOGY

The Picos de Europa have been formed from one of the largest masses of mountain limestone in Europe. Some 350 million years ago, sedimentation processes generated layers of Carboniferous limestone up to 1000m thick in places. The Hercynian orogeny, the collision of the European and African tectonic plates, faulted, folded and elevated the rock mass, superimposing layers of limestone one on top of another. A second major period of mountain building, the Alpine orogeny, then rejuvenated the rocks of the Picos de Europa some 50 million years ago.

The direction of these geological movements folded the limestone strata in a way that gave rise to a predominance of steep south faces over gentler northern slopes. This effect is clearly visible in the Liébana and Valdeón valleys along the southern edge of the Picos de Europa, whilst higher up in the range huge south-facing walls are common, the most imposing of these being that of Peña Santa de Castilla.

There are steep north faces in the Picos, too, but these are the product of glaciation, a much more recent geological phenomenon. During the Quaternary period, which began some 2.6 million years ago, glacial ice completely covered the north of Spain, coming down to as low as 600m above sea level in places. Most of the major high-mountain landscape features of the Picos de Europa, from

Canalizos in the Vega de Liordes (Walks 21 and 22); the effects of karstification are clearly visible to the north of the Jou de la Canal Parda (Walk 8)

deep circular depressions to great vertical walls, owe their current form to glacial action in one way or another. In addition, the main glaciers formed long tongues that carved out valleys that would later become the gorges of the rivers Deva, Duje, Cares and Sella.

The last of the glaciers disappeared some 10,000 years ago, at which point a third geological phenomenon got to work. Karstification is the process through which limestone rock is dissolved away by slightly acidic rainwater. Its effects are spectacular and wide ranging. Water collecting in old glacial cirques dissolved through the bedrock and drained away into the underlying limestone to create a complex of sinkholes, galleries and caves. Some caves systems are over 1500m deep, making the Picos the 'Himalaya' of caving. At the same time, surface-level drainage from rainfall and meltwater, cut into the U-shaped, glacial valleys, creating deep V-shaped grooves in the floor of

each. These V-cuts form the lower sections of the dramatic gorges (*gargantas* or *desfiladeros*) that slice through the Picos from south to north.

Karstification has also left dry and lifeless hollows called *hoyos* or *jous*, a major feature of the Picos mountain landscape. Occasionally these become clogged up, and any water entering forms tarns and small lakes, such as the two above Covadonga. These lakes are not permanent, however, and slowly fill with aquatic vegetation to leave a marshy, heavily vegetated flat area known as a *polje*. The Vega de Liordes in the Central Massif and the Vega de Comeya in the Western Massif are excellent examples of this phenomenon. Finally, karstification is evident on a far smaller scale in the form of *canalizos*, the myriad channels and groves weathered into rocks and slabs throughout the range.

CLIMATE AND WEATHER

Despite lying at the same latitude as Rome, the Picos de Europa enjoy a broadly temperate climate due to the Atlantic fronts that sweep across the whole of Spain's Cantabrian coast for most of the year. On colliding with the mountains, these frontal systems generate the rainfall that makes the Costa Verde so green.

Fortunately, most of the rain falls in the winter and spring, with the period from May to late October being reasonably dry. May, June and July usually offer significant spells of fine weather, and September and October can yield periods of cooler, stable weather ideal for walking. The first snows normally arrive around the end of October, although climate change over the last 20 years has affected all weather patterns, producing higher daytime temperatures and more violent bouts of rain or snow.

The distribution of the rainfall throughout the range is of particular interest when choosing a valley base or looking for a poor-weather activity. As the frontal systems arrive mainly from the north and northwest, the weather on the northern side of the Picos is cooler and wetter on average when compared to the south and southeast of the range. The Liébana and Valdeón valleys benefit from a marked rain-shadow effect, and as a result enjoy noticeably better weather than the valleys on the Asturian side of the range. Sajambre also suffers the effects of incoming Atlantic fronts less than the valleys to the north.

One of the most spectacular weather effects in the Picos is that of an immense sea of cloud filling the valleys to heights of up to 1800m. Surprisingly,

Clockwise from top left: Martagon lily; marsh orchid; white asphodel; blue aconite or wolfsbane; yellow gentians

this is a sign of stable, good weather. An anticyclone over the Azores creates a light, northerly airstream. Warm, moist air drifts in from the Bay of Biscay and fills the northern valleys with a thick, wetting mist known locally as *orbayu*. It is not uncommon to walk up from the valley shrouded in mist and then suddenly come out into bright sunshine. Because of this, it is important to take into account the origin of cloud masses when trying to interpret their significance. This is especially true if you are staying in the Cangas de Onís or Cabrales sectors to the north of the range. Here, it is all too easy to abandon a route early in the day, or never even to leave the valley, because of failing to distinguish between mist and cloud generated by high and low pressure.

PLANTS AND FLOWERS

Huge height variations, fertile valley bottoms, bare rock walls and gorges, mainly basic but occasionally acidic soils, the influence of both Atlantic and Mediterranean climates – with so many factors at play, the vegetation of the Picos de Europa is rich and varied.

Between 200m and 800m (the Coline belt) the dominant feature is mixed, deciduous woodland, principally oak and ash, but also hazel, lime, chestnut and walnut. Beneath

the tree canopy you find plants that thrive in the shade, including wood anemones, hellebores, primroses and the highly attractive martagon lily. At these same altitudes, centuries of clearance have left a mixture of hay meadows and pastures for grazing. These grasslands are home to a huge range of plants, including over 40 species of wild orchid. The spectacular white asphodel is abundant, and its common name in Spanish, *gamón*, gives its name to Gamonedo cheese.

To the north of the Picos, the wetter valleys of Asturias are home to marshland species such as ragged robin, louseworts, globe flowers and early marsh orchids, whilst to the south the drier meadows of the Liébana area are populated by Mediterranean species such as tassel hyacinths. For botanists the switch between these two quite different plant groups makes for fascinating walking.

Further up in the Montane belt from 900 to 1800m, the dominant tree species initially is beech. The extensive beech woods found on the humid, north-facing slopes of the upper Liébana valley and the southern slopes of Valdeón and Sajambre, are one of the prime justifications of National Park status that the Picos de Europa now enjoys. Other tree species at these altitudes include oak lower down, and rowan, birch or holly on the edges of the beech woods, where competition for light is not so fierce.

The Montane belt also refers to the high pastures where livestock graze

throughout the summer. Here you find plants that are able to deal with late, cool summers, including spring and trumpet gentians, tiny wild narcissus, delicate dog's tooth violets, yellow gentians, and the tall but highly poisonous monkshood aconite, known locally as *matalobos* (wolf-killer). The early summer also sees swathes of blue irises (*Iris latifolia*), whilst the late summer sees the appearance of the apparently leafless *Merendera montana*, which tells farmers that it is time to take livestock back down to the valleys. Finally, early autumn sees the high pastures carpeted with pale purple autumn crocuses.

At around 1600m, trees are replaced by scrub made up of juniper, ling, gorse and broom. But the subalpine limestone soils are also home from late spring to early autumn to over 500 plant species. This is over a quarter of all plant species in the Picos de Europa. In the summer there are wonderful displays of stonecrops, saxifrages and toadflaxes, and you should be able to find good examples of yellow gentians and the mountain houseleek. Finally, in the alpine belt above approximately 2200m, soils deep enough for plants to survive are non-existent, and vegetation is more or less restricted to lichens.

WILDLIFE

Wildlife in the Picos de Europa, at least in terms of sightings by the average walker, is limited to just a few

species. Yes, the tourist literature will wax lyrical about wolves and brown bears, but it is highly unlikely that you will see either. If you are lucky, you might you see deer, a fox or wild boar, which might sound a bit tame, but for me never is. However, once into the high mountains you would be very unlucky if you weren't to see *rebeco*, the sturdy little chamois that is so totally at home in the alpine terrain of the Picos and is often spotted grazing in groups in high pastures, or dramatically poised on the very edge of the abyss.

It is a similar story with birds. You won't see capercaillie as their numbers are now critically low. You will, in contrast, see buzzards circling overhead at lower altitudes whilst at varying altitudes you will see different eagles, including booted and golden. In the high mountains, you would be unlucky not to see alpine choughs. If you are eating, in fact, they will often land at your feet looking for scraps, almost inviting you to feed them. At the other end of the scale, if you are very, very lucky, you might just see bearded vultures, or lammergeiers. Re-introduced only recently from the Pyrenees, this is the largest of the vultures in the range, the smallest being the orange-faced Egyptian vulture, a summer visitor. Almost guaranteed, on the other hand, are sightings of the large and magnificent griffon vultures. Making use of rising thermals, they glide majestically across Picos skies all year round, as they have done for so long now. Alpine accentors and snow finches are reasonably easy to spot in the high mountains. Finally, if you keep your eye on the rock walls of the middle to high mountain areas, you might be lucky enough to see the black, grey and vermilion flash of the delightful and aptly named wallcreeper.

No less spectacular than the wallcreeper, but much easier to spot, are the butterflies that grace the meadows and high-mountain pastures of the Picos de Europa. With more than 150 species of butterfly identified in the range and its immediate surroundings, the whole area is a lepidopterist's paradise and the target of specialist holidays. Non-specialists can still delight in the different blues and coppers, and even, perhaps, be lucky enough to see the wonderful swallowtail.

Less immediately attractive than mammals, birds or butterflies, are the green lizard and the fire salamander. The first is most likely to be seen on a hot day, even in places as heavily transited as the Cares Gorge and, if you do get to see one, it will not be easily forgotten. Also memorable is the spectacular, black and yellow fire salamander. In stark contrast to the green lizard, this small amphibian is more likely to cross your path when it is raining. Legend has it that the fire salamander is immune to the flames of a fire. We know this is not possible, and the likely explanation is to do with them running away from logs that had been picked up and placed on a fire.

In 1904, Pedro Pidal, the Marquis of Villaviciosa, and Gregorio Pérez, a shepherd from Caín, climbed El Naranjo de Bulnes for the first time. Fourteen years later, Pidal, a senator in the Spanish parliament, successfully presented the legislation that would lead to the creation of Spain's first national park, the Parque Nacional de la Montaña de Covadonga. The creation of the park coincided with the 1200th anniversary of the Battle of Covadonga, a key moment in Spanish history, but for reasons hard to grasp today, the protection of park status was restricted to the Western Massif, and not extended to the Central and Eastern Massifs.

The inauguration of the cable car at Fuente Dé in 1966 heralded the arrival of modern tourism to the Picos de Europa, which, by the 1980s, were at risk of being swallowed up by an increasingly voracious industry: more cable cars, bigger huts, wider paths, easier access. Suddenly everything was up for grabs, or so much was there to be protected, depending on your point of view.

In the autumn of 1985, a battle began between conservation groups led by the Colectivo Montañero por la Defensa de los Picos de Europa, and the three regional governments, who in turn were aided by private groups interested in exploiting the potential of the range at any cost. For once common sense prevailed, and in 1995 Central Government in

Fuente Dé, a huge, south-facing glacial cirque (Walks 21–25)

Madrid passed the bill that brought the Parque Nacional de los Picos de Europa into existence. With the inclusion of all three massifs in the new park, the area protected jumped overnight from almost 17,000 to almost 65,000 hectares. The addition of part of Peñamellera Alta in 2014 brought the park to its current size of 67,000 hectares (670km²).

The geology and the spectacular landscapes, the vast sweeps of ancient oak and beech woodlands, the rich and varied wildlife, and the immensely beautiful flora – there are many good reasons for bestowing National Park status on the Picos. But these highly tangible motivations tend to overshadow a less obvious attraction. For centuries, shepherding has fashioned so much of what today thrills us as we explore the Picos de Europa. Many of the walks in the range make full or partial use of the intricate network of paths and drove roads that developed to serve the needs of the shepherds and their flocks. The names of so many of the paths, passes and peaks came about in response to the needs of the shepherding community, and were later handed on to the map-makers of the 19th and 20th centuries. And, of course, so much of the deeper, less-immediate beauty of the Picos would simply not exist if the shepherds and their flocks had not made these mountains their home.

Without the seasonal transhumance of livestock from the valleys to the summer pastures, many centuries-old paths would quickly be so overgrown as to be unusable. Without shepherding there would be no hay meadows in the valleys or pastures in the mountains. Without these meadows and pastures, most of the flowers, and as a consequence the insects and butterflies that feed upon them, would not be here.

The cows, goats, sheep and sheepdogs that you will encounter

Sheep farming has contributed so much to the Picos de Europa; the asturiana del monte *breed of cattle is well suited to alpine terrain*

on your walks in the Picos de Europa, are not just appealing foreground detail for photographs. They are keystones to a complex, interconnected living mountain system. In the years to come, the health of the Picos de Europa National Park will be inextricably linked to the extent to which the management plans being put in place today are able to entice tomorrow's generation of young people back to the tough but critical task of farming the Picos.

GETTING THERE

Access to the Picos de Europa from the UK or Europe is not difficult, and can be made either by air or by road through France. From the UK it is also possible to travel to Spain by ferry.

By Road
For three or four people in a car this is an economical approach and solves problems of transport around the range once you are in the Picos. Cross the Franco-Spanish border at Hendaye/Irún. From there, a good

motorway takes you to the Picos de Europa in three to four hours.

By Sea
Brittany Ferries currently run twice-weekly services from Plymouth or Portsmouth to Santander (www.brittany-ferries.co.uk) and three times a week from Portsmouth to Bilbao.

By Air
The closest airports to the Picos de Europa are those of Asturias (OVD), Santander (SDR) and Bilbao (BIO). There are currently direct flights to one or other of these airports from the UK, Germany and Italy. In the absence of a direct flight, you will need to travel via Barcelona or Madrid. A search engine such as Skyscanner (www.sky-scanner.net) is the best way to get up-to-date information on flights.

GETTING AROUND

Bus services in and around the Picos de Europa are not good, with the exception of the summer service from Cangas de Onís to Covadonga, and from there on up to the Covadonga lakes. Much less frequent is the service between Cangas de Onís and Arenas de Cabrales on the north side of the range, or the service from Panes to Potes and then on to Fuente Dé on the south side. In short, it pays to have your own transport in order to be able to move around freely.

LANGUAGE AND MONEY

European Spanish is spoken everywhere, although people in the villages in Asturias might mix this with their local language, Asturiano. In hotels, hostels, restaurants and many bars, somebody will speak some English. In an increasing number of places young members of catering and hotel staff will speak fairly good English. Sadly, English is nowhere near as present as it should be in websites, both private and institutional, though whenever possible I have given links to the English-language version of key texts.

The currency in Spain is the euro. Credit cards, contactless and

Reaching the Collao Pambuches (Walk 32) with the Central Massif behind

conventional, are used for many types of payment in shops, supermarkets, hotels, restaurants and for online booking of mountain huts. However, cash is still the norm in bars and cafés. Payment through phone apps has not caught on yet to any significant extent but is still possible where credit cards are accepted. There are cashpoint machines in all the major towns around the range, although a UK bank may charge you for the service in addition to what you might be charged by the Spanish bank.

WHERE TO STAY

Most of the walks in the guidebook can be done in a day, allowing you to return to a comfortable valley base each night. There is accommodation to fit all pockets in the valleys surrounding the Picos, from luxury hotels to simple hostels (*albergues*), and from self-catering cottages to cabins on campsites. In addition, some towns, such as Posada de Valdeón, have official camper-van parking with full facilities.

Today most travellers use the internet to find their accommodation. Apart from web giants like Booking. com, a small number of sites specialise in accommodation in the Picos de Europa. Most of the available accommodation, however, is found on Spanish sites, not all of which have English-language versions. Regardless of the origin of a website, be careful about the exact location of your accommodation. Some sites use a generous definition of the Picos de Europa and offer rentals that are a significant distance by car from the start of the walks. As a rough guide, anything that lies outside the area covered by the overview map at the front of the book is probably too far away.

For longer walks or for strategic reasons, you may want to stay in one of the mountain huts. This is the case for Walks 7, 8, 15, 16, 35 and 36, whilst for Walk 18 and for the four treks, using the huts makes a lot of sense. Full details of the huts in the Picos can be found in Appendix C, and whilst they are not of the hotel-like standards of those in the Alps (thankfully), the refuges in the Picos de Europa offer meals and accommodation at reasonable prices. All nine huts currently operate through a centralised booking system (https://reservarefugios.com/en) and will require payment in advance. It is essential to use the booking system in July and August in order to guarantee a place. Most wardens speak some English.

WHEN TO VISIT

Depending on the routes you hope to follow, there is no closed season for the Picos de Europa. Valley walks can be done in mid-winter, and even if there is snow in the high mountains, this only adds to the scenery. However, for many visitors from the UK or the rest of Europe, the season running from early May to the end of October is probably the best.

For botanists and plant-lovers in general, there can be little doubt: May and June are the two best months because of the almost overwhelming abundance of flowers both down in the valleys, and higher up in the middle-mountain pastures. Double the guidebook's suggested walk times if you are a flower person and bring a camera capable of decent macro.

These same two months are also good for venturing into the high mountains, although a degree of caution needs to be exercised with any remnants of winter snow. As a minimum, parties venturing above 1500m in May and June, and some years even into July, should carry ice-axes and possibly crampons, and the skill set required to use them safely.

By mid-July and August, the high mountains have shed the last of the snow and are open to all who are willing to make the effort. But be sure to carry enough water and know where springs are; even at 2000m it can get very hot in mid-summer. In addition, always carry a good waterproof, hat and gloves. Mid- and late-summer afternoons can end in thunderstorms which, quite apart from the fear factor, will give you a good soaking.

The weather usually cools off and calms down in September and October. However, early autumn nights can be decidedly cool, and of course the days are shorter than in high summer, although still long enough to do the routes in this guide.

Walking in the Picos is perfectly possible from November through to April if you do not go much above

The enormous south face of Peña Santa de Castilla (Walk 36)

1300m. The days are short and the weather is colder, but anybody used to winter walking in the UK and Europe will have no problems with walks at lower altitudes, and will be rewarded with much clearer air and stunning views of the high summits draped in a dazzling mantle of snow.

WHAT TO TAKE

Equipment is a very subjective affair, but in terms of footwear, for example, modern lightweight boots are ideal for the rough, high-mountain terrain as long as they have good shock-absorbing properties. For valley-level and mid-mountain walks, where the paths and tracks are good underfoot, quality trail running shoes will usually be enough.

The summer in the UK and Europe is also a fair guide as to clothing. Above 1500m, a summer's day in the Picos can be debilitatingly hot or desperately cold, or both. Shorts and T-shirts can seem like a good idea, but can be woefully inadequate in bad weather, and also in very strong sunshine. Full-length trousers and long-sleeved, baggy cotton shirts are a wiser choice. Add a wide-brimmed sun hat and Factor 50 sun cream and you should be ok for the good weather.

Poor weather is more problematical. When it rains, it can rain hard, but you can also find yourself enveloped in a fine, wetting mist known on the Asturian side of the Picos as *orbayu*.

Breathable waterproofs are the sensible option and, as noted earlier, they should go with you everywhere unless the weather is guaranteed fine by a reliable weather app or professional meteorological service.

Whatever the time of year, a compass, a head-torch, emergency food, a small first-aid kit, a lightweight duvet, a dry thermal vest, dry socks and a bivi bag, go with me everywhere, save on the simpler valley walks. A water bottle is essential since water in the high mountains is limited to springs, some of which are not easy to find. I have never been sick from drinking water from springs and drinking troughs.

MAPS

When I wrote the 1989 Cicerone guide to *Walks and Climbs in the Picos de Europa*, mapping was a real problem. Thankfully this is no longer true and excellent paper and digital maps now cover the range. At the time of writing, and based on my own experience as a regular user, the best maps are:

Paper maps
Editorial Alpina, Picos de Europa Parque Nacional, 1:25,000
www.editorialalpina.com/en
An almost obligatory purchase, this excellent map is already in its second edition. The level of detail and accuracy is outstanding, and the two maps, one for the Eastern and Central

massifs and a second for the Western, come in a simple wallet with data for contacting mountain refuges and selected hostels in the valleys. To a very large extent, the place names and the heights used in this guidebook coincide with those given on the Alpina maps.

Adrados Ediciones, Parque Nacional de los Picos de Europa, Mapa topográfica excursionista con la reseña de los itinerrarios de Pequeño y Gran Recorrido (PR y GR) 1:50,000
An excellent publication covering the whole of the national park and a number of areas beyond in a single map that shows all the national park waymarked footpaths, both long-distance (GR) and short distance (PR). It also shows a number of local government waymarked footpaths that fall within the scope of this guidebook. The map is the perfect complement to the Alpina 1:25,000 maps, although the 1:50,000 scale has limitations for walking in the high Picos. Purchase in shops once in the Picos or try online from specialists such as Cordee or Stanfords.

Digital maps
Bob Boulan, Picos de Europa
http://boulan.blogspot.com (and go to Adquirir el mapa)
The best digital map of the Picos and, at 6€ per download, almost a freebie. A vector topographic map that was started in 2004 for personal use and has undergone multiple improvements since then. The map can be downloaded to a desktop computer via Garmin Base Camp, or used on a handheld Garmin GPS device. In the preparation of the GPX files that accompany this guide, I regularly used the Boulan map in order to verify distances and heights in edited GPX files.

GPS IN THE PICOS

Over these last few years, the benefits of GPS when it works have become apparent to me, as have the problems when it doesn't. The benefits hardly need stating, but the vertical cliffs, gorges and woods make the Picos too steep for GPS to be fully reliable. The very real problems encountered with GPS in the Picos also include:

- GPS heights are not as accurate as GPS distances.
- GPS values for the same place can be significantly different at the end of the day compared to the beginning.
- Different GPS devices taken on the same walk by the same person produce different readings (distance, height) and tracks.
- Parameters from the same GPX file show different values (heights, distances, etc) when opened on different digital maps, or when viewed in different editing software.
- High walls, buildings or dense foliage 'blind' the GPS device to the satellite system. It then goes

wild trying to locate a reliable signal, which can generate seriously incorrect readings.

• The same high walls, buildings or woodland foliage mean that even if you have an accurate GPX file uploaded to your device at the beginning of the day, when actually walking in the Picos you cannot always get a reliable signal. In places like the Cares Gorge, this can place you off the path when it is abundantly obvious that you are on it.

In short, although I have done my best to ensure that the GPX files that come with this guidebook are as accurate as possible, you need to take a paper map with you, and you need to know how to use it in combination with a reliable compass.

GPX tracks

GPX tracks for the routes in this guidebook are available to download free at www.cicerone.co.uk/536/GPX. If you have not bought the book through the Cicerone website, or have bought the book without opening an account, please register your purchase in your Cicerone library to access GPX and update information.

We provide files in a single standard GPX format that works on most devices and systems, but you may need to convert files to your preferred format using a GPX converter such as gpsvisualizer.com or one of the many other apps and online converters available.

ROADS, TRACKS AND PATHS

Throughout the guide I have tried to use terms that reflect the terrain each walk is following. This sort of information is shown in excellent detail on the Editorial Alpina maps. A road, then, is tarmacked. A jeep track is something that a tractor, a 4WD vehicle and even a car can be driven along. A track is not apt for most vehicles, and is usually a drove road or rough track used to take livestock up and down to high pastures. A path is something that can only be followed on foot, and often only by people or animals travelling in single file.

Paths in the high mountains can be vague and are especially hard to locate if they cross large slabs of rock. On these occasions, look out for the brownish staining made by mud on the soles of walkers' boots. Tiny cairns will also guide you across trackless terrain, but you need to keep your eyes skinned at all times. Cairns are the same colour as the surrounding rock and may be no more than five or six stones organised into a tiny pyramid. If the guidebook description indicates cairns and you can't see any, backtrack until you find the last sure section of the walk, and then try again, especially when caught in mist or thick cloud.

Red, green, blue or yellow paint dots have survived from earlier, more primitive attempts to waymark routes, especially those that enter high-mountain terrain. Signposts have

Cares Gorge (Walk 33)

replaced paint dots to a large extent up to around 1500m, and the national park waymarked routes, both short distance (PR) and long distance (GR), are all well signed in that respect, making navigation straightforward. When upright signposts are not appropriate, yellow-and-white (PR) and red-and-white (GR) horizontal bars have been painted onto prominent rocks or walls.

July and August are busy months in the Picos and it is unlikely that you will be alone in the mountains. The opposite is true for the rest of the year, and with coverage for mobile phones patchy to poor, you would be very unwise to venture into the Picos alone or in poor weather. Rescue services are very good (see below) but the complex terrain means that it could be days before they find you, by which time you will be dead. Unnecessary deaths over the last few years confirm that this last comment is not an exaggeration, so always leave details of your intended route with friends or family. Go properly equipped, and equip yourself for an emergency.

EMERGENCIES

Mountain rescue in Spain is at the same level as it is in other European countries, and, more importantly, is free at the time of writing in 2022. Nonetheless, if you are visiting Spain from the UK, it would be wise to have insurance, including the cost of rescue by helicopter. Now that the UK is no longer in the EU, you should also take out general travel insurance that covers the cost of medical treatment while in Spain.

In the event an accident, or should someone go missing, the course of action to take will depend on the where you are. In the valleys or middle mountains, either ring 112 (the emergency number throughout Spain) or contact the Guardia Civil (Civil Guard) directly on 062.

In the high mountains, assuming you have a signal for your mobile phone, ring 112. If you cannot get a signal, send a member of the group to the nearest hut. The warden will alert the rescue services by radio and/or organise first aid for the victim where necessary. See Appendix B for

Spanish words and phrases useful in an emergency.

USING THIS GUIDE

So that you have a really positive experience when walking in the Picos, this guide provides you with a good idea of what to expect on each walk, both in the route information box and the route introduction. In addition, routes can be compared in the route summary table.

Key factors when choosing a route are distance, and height gain or loss. Of the two, pay most attention to the latter. A significant number of walks seem to cover a relatively short distance, but on closer inspection are found to involve more than 1000m of ascent. Height gained will need to be lost. Descents in the Picos are frequently steep and stony, and can be on exposed paths cut into sheer rock walls.

The other major factors determining the seriousness of a walk are the terrain and any issues of navigation that come with that terrain, especially above 1500m. In the high mountains some walks follow vague or inexistent paths with only small cairns to guide you, or cross featureless slabs of rock that can be difficult to navigate in poor weather.

With these factors in mind, the walks have been graded as Easy, Moderate, Difficult or Very difficult, broadly based on the considerations detailed below.

Heading up to the Ándara hut from the Joyu del Teju car park (Walk 15)

The route descriptions are concise but precise, giving enough detail for you to be able to follow the walk without the need to use a GPS device. Included in each route description at various points are values for the distance walked up to that point, and the altitude. However, there are no timings for individual sections of a route. This is because timings can vary wildly depending on level of fitness, motivation on a given day, stops to take notes, to look at maps, for photography…

The times given in the data box for each route are calculated from a

Grade	Distance	Height gain	Terrain	Route finding
Easy	Under 10k	Under 400m	Good paths and tracks throughout. Neither steep nor exposed.	Obvious, with lots of waymarking.
Moderate	10–15k	400–800m	Mostly on good paths and tracks. Occasionally steep and/or exposed.	Mostly easy with good waymarking.
Difficult	15–20k	800–1100m	Some trackless uneven ground. Quite often steep and/or exposed	Poor waymarking over some sections.
Very difficult	Over 20k	Over 1100m	Trackless, broken ground. Often very steep and exposed.	Often complex with little waymarking

At the Mirador de Ordiales, the site of
the tomb of Pedro Pidal (Walk 6)

combination of distance and height gain/loss. The estimated time given in the introduction to a walk is based on travelling at roughly 4km/h and ascending or descending at 300m/h. These are not brilliant speeds, but they are good enough in the middle and high-mountain terrain of the Picos. If you time yourself over a couple of walks you can then adjust this formula to fit your pace. Above all, however, give yourself plenty of time. Trail runners will dash past you in the more popular areas of the Picos, T-shirted and in shorts, and carrying little more than water. But the walks in this guidebook are not to be run. They are to be walked. They are to be enjoyed. Relished for what they offer. Savoured to the full. All that takes time.

CANGAS DE ONÍS

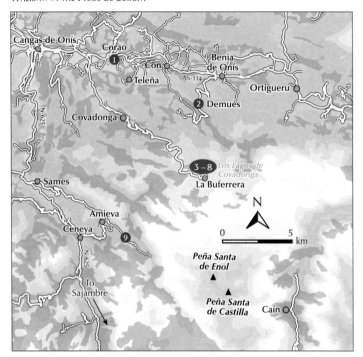

The walks in the Cangas de Onís sector all lie in the Western Massif, with a good number of them starting out quite high up at the Lagos de Covadonga, one of the foremost destinations for visitors to the Picos. From there, a number of routes venture up into the high mountains, although almost always on paths that are not as steep as those in the other sectors. This can make some of these outings attractive to less experienced walkers.

Cangas de Onís, the main town in the sector, offers all the services you would expect, including banks, supermarkets, shops, a post office, and a tourist information office. Cangas makes an excellent base for routes not just in the immediate area, but also in the Cabrales and Sajambre sectors. On the down side, because it is popular, Cangas de Onís can be quite crowded during the summer season. In that respect, accommodation in the villages along the valley of the River Güeña as far as Benia and Avín are, for me, of greater use to visiting mountaineers. There is a huge

The two Peñas Santas from near Lago Enol, with the Torre de Santa María on the right (Walk 3)

range of accommodation, including good campsites in both Soto de Cangas and Avín.

An interesting town in its own right, Cangas de Onís offers easy access to the historical complex at Covadonga, which is a must for visitors to the Picos. Of special relevance to anybody interested in the wildlife of the Picos de Europa are:

- **El Centro 'Las montañas del Quebrantahuesos'**. The Centre is dedicated to the recovery of the lammergeier (bearded vulture) in the Picos, but explores the way in which traditional shepherding interacts with presence of these magnificent birds. https://quebrantahuesos.org/the-mountains-of-the-lammergeier-centre/?lang=en
- **El Centro de Interpretación de la Fauna Glacial de los Picos de Europa**. A large natural cave housing an exhibition of the fauna that inhabited the Picos de Europa 45,000 years ago. The nearby Peruyal cave has the authentic fossilized remains of a small rhinoceros.https://www.onisecoturismo.es/planifica/centro-fauna-glacial/

Regular but infrequent bus services connect Cangas de Onís to Benia, Avín, Ortigueru, and on to Cabrales. A bus currently runs once a day from Cangas de Onís to Oseja de Sajambre. There is a regular service to Oviedo. For more details see https://www.alsa.com/en/web/bus/home.

Frequent buses link Cangas de Onís to Covadonga and Los Lagos de Covadonga. The service runs at Easter, at weekends from Easter to the end of May, and daily from June to the end of October. During this period, the road from Covadonga to Los Lagos is closed to private traffic from 8am to 9pm. For updated details of the service see

Covadonga from the Cruz de Priena (Walk 1)

https://www.alsa.es/acceso-autobus-cangas-onis-lagos-covadonga.

To use the service, park and join the buses either in Cangas de Onís, or at any of the well-signed car parks from Soto de Cangas up to Covadonga itself. You can only buy a return ticket, but this is cheap, and if the weather turns nasty once you are at the lakes, you are free to go back down on the bus. Get an early bus to avoid the queues, and sit on the L going up if you are at all nervous on narrow roads with sizeable drops.

Also currently running for one month during the summer is an ALSA company bus service from Cangas de Onís to Posada de Valdeón and the start of the Cares Gorge (Walk 33). Buses then collect walkers at Poncebos and transport them back to Cangas.

Details of taxi services around the Onís sector, especially those up to the Covadonga lakes can be found at https://www.taxitur.es. (Spanish only web). Taxis can provide a good alternative to the bus service to the lakes.

WALK 1
La Cruz de Priena

Start/Finish	Castañeu de Corao (opposite Bar Abamia)
Distance	18km
Ascent/Descent	890m
Grade	Difficult
Time	6–7hr
Terrain	The first half follows the PR-PNPE 1 on good tracks and paths. The upper section follows a narrow path along a broad, airy ridge. Muddy in places.
Map	Adrados Ediciones, 1:50,000. Parque Nacional de los Picos de Europa
Access	From Soto de Cangas follow the AS114 to east to Corao. Park in Corao near the old cattle market area of the Castañeu, opposite Bar Abamia.
Route finding	Some issues

This is a walk that is steeped in ancient history but is also connected to the more recent past of the Picos de Europa. The first half follows the Senda de Frasinelli, the route a 19th-century German romantic followed in his excursions into the Western Massif, but which has been used for centuries to drive livestock up to summer grazing. The second part offers a little-seen, bird's-eye view of the religious complex at Covadonga, some 500m below. The route can be done with a low cloud base, as the highest summit lies below 800m.

Start at the information board on the south side of the stream that delimits the S edge of the **Castañeu de Corao** (0km; 100m). Follow a good track for 1km to reach the small but delightful **Santa Eulalia de Abamia** church (1.3km; 185m).

The **8th-century church** was built to house the remains of Pelayo, the Asturian nobleman who

defeated the Moors in the Battle of Covadonga and in doing so initiated La Reconquista, the Christian Reconquest of Spain. Pelayo and his wife Gaudiosa were buried in the church until the 13th century, when King Alfonso X had their bodies taken to Covadonga.

Soon after the church pass through Cueto Abamia and its scatter of well-kept houses, then climb steeply to gain good views R towards Cangas de Onís and N to Corao. At 2.6km go R and then R again soon after passing between two large cabins. Zig-zig up past the cabins and small houses of **Canal** (3km; 335m). Trees line the jeep track and shelter you from the morning sun, but when they recede you are rewarded with an excellent view N to the village of Teleña. This is best seen from a natural platform with a circular water deposit (4km; 450m). ▸

With climate change, water is becoming a scarce commodity even in Asturias, and the route is littered with dry drinking troughs.

At a junction at 4.3km take the L track, which now levels off and swings E below and due N of the Cruz de Priena summit. At the **Collado Pandal** (5km; 490m) the jeep track swings sharp R and then quickly back L amid mature trees. At Uporquera (5.6km; 550m) the track splits. ▸

The Latin for pig is porcus. Names like Uporquera probably have to do with pigs in one form or another, domestic or wild.

Above to the R at this point is the col that you come down later in the day when you descend from the Priena summit. Ignore this for now, and follow the jeep track steeply down. It ends almost immediately in a clearing with an old cabin on the L (5.8km; 530m). Now follow a good path along the side of a walled field to the R. The section of the route that lies ahead is known as the **Camino del Rey**, and rises gently as it traverses SE across a huge slope of mixed heather, gorse and bracken.

Most of the slopes around you at this point lie over quartzite and sandstone rocks. These give rise to **landforms** that are quite different to those of the limestone that dominates so much of the Picos de Europa.

On reaching an open grassy col (7.6km; 680m) you gain views E to the village of Gamoneu, an area in the Picos rightly famed for its blue cheese. On reaching a second, smaller col, strike up S to gain a third col on the **Sierra de Estaca** ridge. You are at **Tarañodios** (8.2km; 730m) an abandoned *majada*, and for the first time you can now look down towards Covadonga, though you can't quite see it yet. ▸

Churned-up grass on any of these cols is the work of wild boar, which abound in these parts, although they are hard to see during the day.

The Majada de Tarañodios – Cabezu Severa is visible top right

Here the PNPE-PR 1 drops down SE to the CO4 road from Covadonga, but ignore this and turn NW instead. Take in the **Cabezu Severa** summit (8.7km; 771m), which strictly speaking is off-route, but is an excellent place from which to view both the mornings efforts, and the route ahead. This is also a good place to spot griffon vultures, and even a bearded vulture if you are very lucky.

Griffon vultures suffered badly in the 60s and 70s because of the indiscriminate use of pesticides. Their population has recovered since the 1980s thanks to the work of local conservationists. The bearded vulture, or lammergeier, disappeared altogether from the Picos de Europa, but a programme of reintroduction means that they can now be seen throughout the range in small but growing numbers.

The Centro para la Biodiversidad y el Desarrollo Sostenible, just W of Benia on the AS-114, has a good display on the work of the Bearded Vulture Conservation Fund (https://quebrantahuesos.org/) and is an excellent way to use a morning off, or get the best out of part of a rainy day.

From the Cabezu Severa, return the main ridge and follow it on a narrow path. This can be hard to find when it goes through bushes but, in general, it stays on the Covadonga side of the crest. Covadonga itself comes into view unexpectedly and, if the light is right, quite breathtakingly.

After struggling a while longer with bushy scrub, you come to a small col, the Collado el Pasaderu (10.9km; 602m). Climb up NW on the obvious trail to the summit of the **Cruz de Priena** (11.5km; 725m). The views are outstanding in all directions, so take your time; whilst below in Frassinelli's basilica, the faithful seek their place in heaven, up here by the Cruz de Priena, you already have yours.

Born in Germany, **Roberto Frassinelli** was a Romanticist who fled from his native Germany in 1836 for political reasons. His interest in medieval churches led him to Corao, where he settled and married. A great defender of the beauty of the Picos de Europa, he was also a qualified draughtsman and was responsible for the design plans of the neo-Gothic Basilica at Covadonga. This walk unites the

The view from Cabezu Severa with the Camino del Rey below right and the Cruz de Priena top left

three places that were a central pillar to Frassinelli's life – Corao, the Western Massif and Covadonga.

Retrace your steps down to the Collado el Pasaderu. Turn NE and descend to Uporquera, coming out close to where the ascent track zig-zagged down and ended. Follow the jeep track back down to **Corao**. The route is the same as this morning, but the light and your spirits are not; rest and refreshments are waiting for you in Bar Abamia.

WALK 2
La Majada de Belbín

Start/Finish	Demués
Distance	22km
Ascent/Descent	1200m
Grade	Difficult
Time	8–9hr
Terrain	Jeep tracks and well-used paths. Some mud and a road to finish.
Map	Editorial Alpina, 1:25,000. Picos de Europa, Macizo Occidental
Access	From just W of Benia de Onís take the road S through Bobia de Abajo and Bobia de Arriba and on to Demués (5km). There is parking in Demués on the R just after entering the village.
Route finding	Straightforward, except for the section crossing the Vega de Comeya.

The Onís rural district is famous for its excellent Gamonedo cheese (not to be confused with Cabrales cheese from the Central Massif). To make the cheese the shepherds drive their livestock up to the high pastures for the summer. This walk follows one of these drove roads up to the Majada de Belbín, and another one down. In Belbín you can visit a working *majada*, which is a collection of huts where shepherds spend the summer months tending the livestock and making cheese.

From the car park (0km; 425m) walk back along the road to the first houses of **Demués**, where a jeep track leads off SW. This is the start of the PR-PNPE 8, which coincides with the first half of this walk. Follow the track up past

Views of Gamonedo and the Torre de Santa María on leaving Demués

Sometimes steep, the track rewards you throughout with ever-changing views R to the village of Gamonedo de Onís and its mosaic of pastures.

a small chapel and then the village telecommunications tower. ◀

After some steady climbing, a good track leads off and up L (2.7km; 590m). This variation of the PR-PNPE 8 leads up to **Cabañayu**, a disused *majada* with a collection of partially restored circular cabins (4.8km, 780m). An information board provides a description of the cabins, which lie a short distance below.

From Cabañayu follow a rising path south until it is possible to descend back to the main track, at the **Colláu el Reguero** (6km; 770m). From there follow the jeep track to the **Colláu Lincós** (7.2km; 900m). Both cols offer splendid views both down into the Río Casaño gorge and SE to the tortured walls and gullies of Peña Ruana. The vicious ramp that leads away from the Lincós col is short-lived and deposits you right next to the **Mirador de Camba** (7.9km; 1045m).

As soon as you catch sight of the views from the Camba lookout point the ramp will be forgotten. The whole of Onís lies at your feet to the NE, hemmed in to the

S by the dark, forbidding slopes of the Cuesta Rabucán. The silhouette of the Cantón de Texéu fills the foreground to the S, with the elegant Torre de Santa María looming over it in the far distance. The flat-topped, imposing bulk of Torrecerredo, the highest summit in Northern Spain, dominates the Central Massif of the Picos to the SE.

Shortly after the Mirador de Camba the jeep track ends at a small shelter and a park information board (8.5km; 1045m). ▶ This is the point of entry into the national park. A well-made path takes over from the jeep track, skirts round the **Cantón de Texéu** and then descends to the high pastures of the **Vega las Mantegas**, where it ends. Once in the Mantegas meadows it is important to trend R, looking out for low marker posts and for a path that leads steeply up R to a track. ▶ This descends immediately into the delightful **Majada de Belbín** (10km; 1058m).

> With the support of the national park authorities the **Belbín** has been restored as a fully working *majada*. Cheese is still made here and then cured over several months in the limestone caves in the surrounding hills, the bacteria in the caves giving the cheese its unique flavour. Some of the buildings in the *majada* are obviously shepherd's huts, whilst others are for livestock. In the *tendayos* type of cabin, the sheep and goats shelter in the upper floor, the cows staying on the ground floor. A mixture of cow, sheep and goat's milk is one of the defining characteristics of Gamonedo cheese.

Take a good track, leave the SE corner of Belbín and work your way W before veering sharp R (N) after climbing up to a broad ridge with excellent views of both Torrecerredo and the Torre de Santa María, as well as the ever-popular Ercina and Enol lakes. ▶ Follow the track N then NW to the **Pedro Pidal visitor centre** (13km; 1070m) which, when open, provides valuable information about the national park in general, and the mine workings in the area in particular. ▶

Soñín de Arriba, a working majada, lies off to the E and is well worth exploring in the summer months.

There are plans to extend the existing track from the point where it enters the national park to the Majada de Belbín.

Mere tarns compared to lakes elsewhere, the Lagos de Covadonga are a rarity in massifs like the Picos de Europa because of the permeability of limestone rock.

See Walk 3 for more details.

49

A footpath leads away from the N end of the visitor centre and down to the Buferrera car park. Part way down an unsurfaced path (PR-PNPE 1) drops away steeply R and takes you through the Escaleru tunnel and then out above the immense plain of the Vega de Comeya.

The **Escaleru tunnel** was dug as part of the mining operations that were carried out above at the Buferrera (Walk 3). You can still see the remains of the towers from the cableway that transported the mineral down to Comeya in the gorge to the L of the tunnel.

The Escaleru tunnel on the descent into Comeya

Shortly after coming out of the tunnel, there is a signpost for the PR-PNPE 1 which is off L to Corao (13.7km; 920m). Ignore this, and instead descend ENE to gain and then cross the flat, narrow eastern end of the **Vega de Comeya**. Ascend first E and then NE, eventually skirting round below the scatter of abandoned cabins of Soñín d'Abaxu, and from there go almost due E to the broad **Colláu Soñín d'Abaxu** (15.4km; 980m).

Dropping down from the col, pick up the path that descends steadily N and then NW across the upper slopes of the **Cueto Salgaréu**. When the path enters woodland it can be muddy in places, but eventually brings you out at the **Collado Entrepeñas**. Here there is a spring, a drinking trough and the start of a jeep track (17.6km: 690m).

Follow the track comfortably down to the narrow road that connects the hamlets of Gamonéu de Cangas and Gamonéu de Onís to Demués (20km; 360m). Turn R and follow the road back to **Demués**, sparing a thought for the shepherds who in the past thought nothing of doing the whole of this route before lunch.

The Vega de Comeya, with the path up to Soñín d'Abaxu visible in the centre

WALKS FROM LA BUFERRERA

Walks 3–8 all start from the Buferrera car park next to the Covadonga lakes. Access to the car park from Covadonga is via the CO-4 road. The road is not for nervous drivers, and at Easter, during the summer and on Bank Holiday weekends it is closed to private cars from 07:30 to 20:00. At these times access to the Buferrera car park and the lakes is by private taxi (www.taxitur.es), or you can use the frequent local bus services. Buses leave from Cangas de Onís and stop at multiple designated car parks from Soto de Cangas to Covadonga. Tickets can be bought at kiosks at the car parks between Soto and Covadonga, and online at www.alsa.com/en/web/bus/bus-schedules.

WALK 3
La Buferrera and Los Lagos

Start/Finish	La Buferrera car park
Distance	5.9km
Ascent/Descent	200m
Grade	Easy
Time	3hr
Terrain	Good paths or tracks except for the central section, which can be muddy and is on uneven, rocky ground.
Map	Editorial Alpina, 1:25,000. Picos de Europa, Macizo Occidental
Access	See 'Walks from La Buferrera', above.
Route finding	PR-PNPE 2. Good waymarking except in the Palomberu woods.

This is a short, easy walk either for a gentle day or as a poor weather option when it can be combined with Walk 4. Even as a poor weather option, however, what the route lacks in difficulty, it easily makes up for in terms of intrinsic interest. Steeped in history, the route offers constantly changing scenery with superb views on a fine day. It is also an excellent introduction to the geology of limestone and the process of karstification.

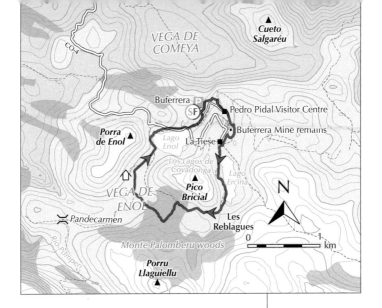

From the upper of the two **Buferrera parking areas** (1040m) follow the signs for the PR-PNPE 2 and the **Centro de Visitantes 'Pedro Pidal'** (0.4km; 1070m). It is well worth stopping here since what is on display will help you understand what you are about to see during the walk.

> **Pedro Pidal**, the Marquis of Villaviciosa, is remembered for two actions, each of which left an indelible mark on the Picos de Europa. The first of these was to push forward the legislation that converted the Western Massif of the Picos into a national park back in 1918, making it the seventh national park in the world. The second was the first ascent of El Naranjo de Bulnes in 1904, accompanied by Gregorio Pérez, a shepherd from Caín. Pedro Pidal's body now lies in a tomb at the Mirador de Ordiales (Walk 6).

From the visitor centre, go up some steps and through the fenced arboretum, with its collection of tree types typical of the Picos de Europa. Come out of the arboretum and head for the **Buferrera mine workings**,

The descent into the Buferrera mine workings

either directly through the old tunnel, or by following the path above and to the R (0.8km; 1080m). Either way, you will reach the heart of the old workings with its curious sculpture, and then follow the path as it winds up through the old workings and past a labyrinth of heavily eroded, limestone formations.

The **Buferrera mines** extracted mostly iron and manganese. The first mine opened in 1868 and the minerals were carried down to Covadonga by men or horses; the existing road up to the lakes from Covadonga was initially built to this end. In 1983 the British company 'Asturiana de Minas Ltd' took over the mine, and ran it until its closure in 1932, a victim of the 1929 stock market crash. The Second World War and the need for manganese, revived the fortunes of La Buferrera, at least until 1958, when things worsened again. The mine finally closed in 1979.

Soon after leaving the Buferrera mine workings, you come to the basin of the **Lago Ercina** and a magnificent view of the main summits of the Western Massif, including the two Peñas Santas (Sacred Peaks), Peña Santa de Enol (or Torre de Santa María) and Peña Santa de Castilla (or Torre Santa).

PEÑAS SANTAS

The Peñas Santas have different names depending on which map you are looking at. The confusion stems from events in September 1891, when the Conde de Saint-Saud attempted to make the first ascent of the Peña Santa de Castilla, which he had seen from the León side of the massif. Approaching from the Lago de Enol in misty weather, the group unintentionally made the first ascent of the Torre de Santa María.

Once on the summit, Saint-Saud saw that he was on the wrong mountain. His Peña Santa clearly lay to the southeast, but when questioned about the confusion, the local guide insisted that they had climbed Peña Santa. Nor was he wrong. Locals in Asturias did in fact refer to the Torre de Santa María as the Peña Santa.

To clarify things, Saint-Saud renamed their summit the Peña Santa de Enol, and began to refer to the other one as the Peña Santa de Castilla. As a result, some current maps use variations on the original names based on those Saint-Saud introduced in 1891.

From the small café at **La Tiese** (1.3km; 1130m), follow the path along the western shore of the Lago Ercina.

The **Ercina lake** is glacial in origin but is now quite shallow due to natural clogging processes. Eventually, it will fill completely, leaving a flat, marshy area as a reminder of what was once here.

From the S end of the lake (2.2km; 1120m), follow the signs for PR-PNPE 2 and climb up briefly to the cabins at the **Les Reblagues** (2.7km; 1130m), then contour W above the depression of the **Vega el Brical**, which is a fine example of what is left after the natural clogging of a small lake is complete. ▶

Now swing NW and cross a rocky area that leads to a junction in the route (3.1km, 1110m). Ignore the R fork and extend the walk a little by heading SW to enter **Monte Palomberu beech woods**. The ground is rocky and uneven, but even in poor weather the beauty of the woods makes up for this. Just when the terrain is trying your patience, the route comes out at the jeep track

In spring the combined rainfall and snowmelt entering the Bricial is greater than its capacity for drainage and a shallow, temporary tarn forms.

55

Mist creeps around the beech woods of Monte Palomberu

that runs from the Lago Enol to the **Pandecarmen** (4km: 1085m). Turn R and follow the track NE across the **Vega de Enol**, a classic middle-mountain grazing area, going past the **Ermita de El Buen Pastor** (the Chapel of the Good Shepherd).

> The Fiesta del Pastor is held in the **Vega de Enol** each year at the end of July. Starting with morning mass, the day involves traditional music and dancing, bare-back horse-riding, and a foot race to the summit of the nearby Porra de Enol (1279m). On the more serious side, there is a meeting of the Consejo de Pastores (Shepherds' Council) in order to deal with grazing rights, and to elect the new *Regidor* (Head Shepherd).

On leaving the Vega de Enol the track swings NE and you get an excellent view of the **Lago Enol** (4.8km; 1080m).

Over 20m deep in places, and with obvious glacial origins, the Lago Enol represents the beginning of the clogging process that will eventually leave it looking like the Vega el Bricial. In one short walk you have seen all three geological stages of lake formation and filling in an area of limestone karst.

Follow the track briefly NW, then drop down R and skirt round the north shore of the lake along a narrow path. On reaching the point where the lake drains out (5.9km; 1040m), take the road down to the **Buferrera car park** and the end of a short but fulfilling walk.

WALK 4

Covadonga from Los Lagos

Start	La Buferrera car park
Finish	Covadonga
Distance	10.5km
Ascent	280m
Descent	1065m
Grade	Moderate
Time	3–4hr
Terrain	Mostly rough paths. Slippery if wet. Not well signed.
Map	Editorial Alpina, 1:25,000. Picos de Europa, Macizo Occidental
Access	See 'Walks from La Buferrera', above.
Route finding	Straightforward. Some care needed over the section from Fana to Les Mestes.

The pool below the Holy Cave at Covadonga is fed by the Les Mestes stream, which disappears into a spectacular cave mouth higher up in the Vega de Orandi. This short walk descends from the Lagos de Covadonga via a sequence of lonely *vegas* (mountain meadows) that lead to Les Mestes and Orandi. The route is easily combined with Walk 3, and so is a good option when the weather is doubtful higher up in the mountains.

Leave the **Buferrera car park** (1040m) by the NE corner on a good path, but almost immediately drop down L on

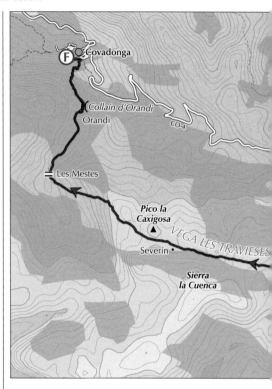

a much more rudimentary path, signed the PR-PNPE 1 to Comeya. The path goes past a pylon from the old mine cableway, and through a tunnel. Shortly after the tunnel (0.9km) the path broadens. Drop down L here at a sign to Corao via the PR-PNPE 1. Descend easily to the old mine spoil heaps that are evident above the huge marshy plain of the **Vega de Comeya** to the N.

> The **cableway** was used to transport raw mineral ore from the Buferrera mine down to settling ponds on the floor of Vega de Comeya. There are three pillars down on the southern slopes of Comeya and

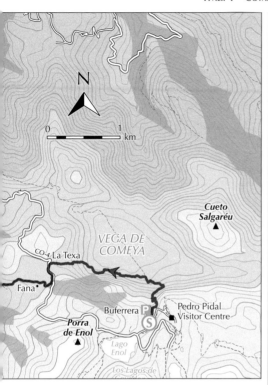

numerous small spoil heaps. Power for the process-
ing plant was supplied by a mini hydroelectric power
station served by water from the Lago Enol. From
Comeya the treated manganese and iron ores were
carried down to Covadonga, initially by ox cart, then
by motor vehicle, and finally, from 1905 on, using
a 7km cableway. From Covadonga the ores were
exported to France, Belgium and England.

Skirt around the Vega de Comeya keeping more or less
along it S edge below steep, wooded walls. From the SW
corner of Comeya strike off W up muddy, gorse-covered

slopes. There is no real path here, but a short struggle uphill takes you to the drinking trough at **La Texa** (2.6km; 960m), and soon after that to the **CO-4 road**.

Turn L and walk S next to the road for 200m, then take the jeep track that goes off R and follow it to where it swings back on itself and drops down SE to **Fana** (3.8km; 950m). ◄

From the final hairpin on the track strike off W and work your way across gorse-covered slopes below a rocky ridge to gain the R-hand end of a broad, tree-covered col (4.9km; 995m). From the col begin your descent to Covadonga. Go first across the twin meadows of the **Vega les Travieses**, and then climb briefly to a broad, grassy col (Spot Height 889m). Descend from the col until level with the two ruined cabins of **Severín**, then descend slightly R towards a rocky pyramidal summit (**Pico la Caxigosa**, 896m). ◄

Keeping the Caxigosa summit on your R, descend NW over gorse-covered slopes. When these finally die out (what a relief!) open pastures lead comfortably down past a sign for the PR-PNPE 6 (7.6km; 700m), and on still further down to the tiny bridge at **Les Mestes** (8.2km; 570m). Stay on the true R bank of the river and follow this across increasingly overgrown meadows to **Orandi** (9.2km; 530m). The visit to the mouth of the cave is obligatory; the same waters that disappear so suddenly from view here, reappear below in Covadonga at the spot where the walk ends.

The sudden disappearance and re-appearance of rivers in the Picos de Europa is typical of any major limestone area. In a process known as **karstification**, slightly acid rainwater has dissolved away the rock to create an extensive network of caves and underground water courses. Although the effect of karstification is often spectacular when these underground waters re-appear, the process has one serious implication for all mountaineers. This is the need to locate springs successfully in the high mountains, or to risk going thirsty all day.

In good weather the northern peaks of the Western Massif gradually appear to the S as you descend to Fana.

By June these meadows are home to herds of cows, the most common breed being the Asturiana del Monte or Casina. With its striking, chestnut coat and wide, opening horns, these hardy cows bring life to the mountain pastures all over Asturias.

The cave at Orandi

From Orandi, follow the path briefly up through woods to the **Collaín d'Orandi**. From here descend steeply on often slippery ground to come out suddenly onto a cobbled lane (10.4km; 260m). Turn L here and in 100m enter **Covadonga** at the esplanade immediately below the Holy Cave, with its tiny chapel and the much-revered statue of La Santina. It is traditional on visiting Covadonga to drink from the Fuente de los Siete Caños at the back of the pool below the Holy Cave.

WALK 5
Ario and El Jultayu

Start/Finish	La Buferrera car park
Distance	19.6km; (22.1km for Vegas del Gamonedo variant)
Ascent/Descent	1275m (1715m for Vegas del Gamonedo variant)
Grade	Very difficult
Time	7–9hr
Terrain	Good path to the Vega de Ario. Difficult from Ario to the summit (difficult from Ario to Vega Maor for the Vegas del Gamonedo variant).
Map	Editorial Alpina, 1:25,000. Picos de Europa, Macizo Occidental
Access	See 'Walks from La Buferrera', above.
Route finding	Straightforward. Waymarked to the *refugio*. Waymarking and cairns to the summit.

Even without tackling El Jultayu, the walk to the Vega de Ario is well worth the effort. Few places can boast the sort of majestic views that reward your efforts when you reach El Jitu. Ario itself is delightful, and a terrible temptation to stop and relax. But if you make the extra effort and go to the summit of the Jultayu, then the day will be truly memorable. The view down to Caín almost 1500m below is not easily forgotten.

From the E end of the **Buferrera car park** (1040m) follow PR-PNPE 2 up to the **Pedro Pidal visitor centre** and then on past the old mine workings and so up to **Lago Ercina** (1.1km; 1120m) and views of the northern summits of the Western Massif. Cross the meadow to the E of the lake and pick up the PR-PNPE 4 path, which is visible skirting round below the W walls of **Pico Llucia**. Follow the path past cabins, then climb gently up to more open ground and gain a broad col with good views of the Torrecerredo group in the Central Massif in the far distance (3km; 1293m). Descend to **Las Bobias** (3.8km; 1250m), where

El Jitu offers dramatic views of the Central Massif

just beyond the **shepherds' cabins** there is an unusual spring welling from a large rock. This is the last drinkable water until Ario. ▶

From the spring, climb away R with surprising views N to the Bay of Biscay, then cross rocky ground above the upper reaches of the Redondiella valley on the L. Cross the tiny stream at the head of the valley (4.6m; 1270m), and then climb steeply up following the obvious zig-zags. The path continues to climb, winding its way up the **Valle las Campizas**, where more open ground offers views of the Cuvicente and Verdilluengua summits to the SE. A final steeper section leads to **El Jitu** (7.3km; 1650m), a broad shoulder. ▶

Now skirt round L below the Cabeza la Porma and so reach the 'Marqués de Villaviciosa' hut (8km; 1630m), which stands proudly in the back, left corner of the fabulous Vega de Ario. ▶

The **Marqués de Villaviciosa** hut (also known as the Refugio de Ario) was built in 1960 by the local authorities. The name of the hut honours the man who first climbed El Naranjo de Bulnes together with local shepherd, El Cainejo. The two men met

Like Belbín (Walk 2), Las Bobias is an excellent example of a working majada, with numerous traditional cabins for livestock and shepherds.

El Jitu offers sudden, dramatic views of the Torrecerredo and Friero groups in the Central Massif.

The views of the Central Massif in the late evening sun make it well worth spending the night at the Ario hut.

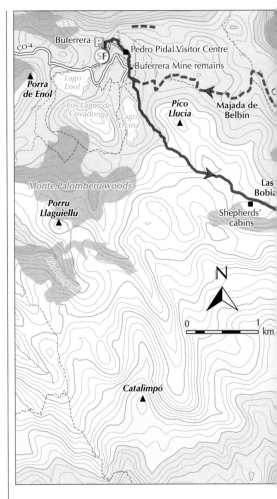

in Ario and spent two nights there before crossing the Cares Gorge and traversing above Bulnes to reach the Majada de Cambureru (Walk 18). The day they spent based in Ario was used to climb

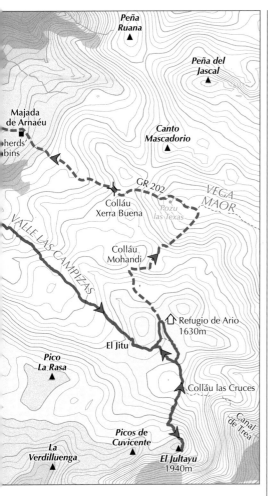

both the Torre de Santa María and Peña Santa de Castilla, neither of which are exactly nearby. The term 'physically fit' doesn't really describe these early pioneers.

To climb El Jultayu, leave the hut on a narrow path going essentially SSE across the meadow. At the bottom end of the meadow, signposts and abundant yellow paint marks lead over uncomfortable limestone pavement. Despite the signing, care is needed to navigate correctly to the broad **Colláu las Cruces** above the entrance to the **Canal de Trea** (9.1km; 1571m). Abandon the Trea path at the col and follow frequent small cairns and an intermittent path S and SW so as to gain the broad N spur of **El Jultayu**. Climb this steeply but in good positions. The intermittent path leads to a very sudden summit (10.4km; 1920m). The descent and the return to the start of the walk is made by reversing the route via Ario and Las Bobias.

> The **view of Caín** from the summit, although stunning, is not for anyone with vertigo. Even for those with a head for heights, it would not be wise to lean too far over the edge towards Caín in windy weather. Much less intimidating, is the ample panorama of the Central Massif, the view S to the lower part of Valdeón, and the superb view down to the path along the Cares Gorge (Walk 33).

Optional descent: Vegas del Gamonedo

If you stay overnight in the Ario hut after your ascent of El Jultayu, you not only get to see the spectacle of the sunset over the Central Massif, but are perfectly situated to return to La Buferrera via some of the most attractive working *vegas* and *majadas* in the whole of the Picos.

Start the optional descent by leaving the Marqués de Villaviciosa hut heading NW on a narrow path. At the col immediately behind the hut take time to work out the route around the W side of the Cabeza las Campanas to the **Colláu Mohandi** (1.1km; 1510m). From the col follow a vague path E down into Mohandi, a tiny, remote *vega* (1.4km; 1470m).

Leave Mohandi via the NE edge and begin the tricky descent to Vega Maor. Do NOT lose sight of the cairns over this section and do be sure to locate a short but very stony gully that descends ESE quite early on (1.8km; 1440m). On arrival in **Vega Maor** (2.6km; 1220m), the route joins the **GR 202**, which crosses the Picos from Covadonga to Cosgaya in three or four superb days' walking (see Trek 4). Turn NW and follow the GR 202 up past the impressive **Pozu las Texas** sink hole, and on to the **Colláu Xerra Buena** (4km; 1427m) with its superb views W and NW to the Covadonga lakes and the eastern coast of Asturias.

PICOS CHEESES AND THE DENOMINACIÓN DE ORIGEN

During the summer months the *majadas* and *vegas* this route visits are in full swing, with cattle, sheep and goats all grazing in and around the little clusters of shepherds' huts, and on beyond up to the very highest pastures. The presence of the three types of livestock is not accidental, since cheeses like Gamonedo and Cabrales require a mixture of all three milks in order to fulfil the strict regulations which govern their commercialisation, and which allow them to qualify for the national certificate of origin and quality known as the Denominación de Origen.

Now descend to the **Majada de Arnaéu** (4.6km; 1270m), yet another working summer pasture, and the site of a good spring with cool, fresh water. From Arnaéu continue WNW with fairly good waymarking and reach a broad, grassy col (7.2km; 1053m) where waymarked routes are signposted off to Demués (PR-PNPE 8), Culiembro (GR 202) and Belbín (GR 202). Follow the grassy track that climbs briefly WNW then descends due S into **Belbín** (7.7km; 1055m), a spectacle in the summer when it is thriving with livestock.

From Belbín, follow a good track up and W to reach a high point next to livestock pens (9.4km; 1155m) shortly after a hairpin bend. Abandon the track and descend over grassy slopes back towards the **Lago Ercina** car park. Pick up the footpaths that lead back to the **Bufarrera car park** (10.5km; 1040m), and the end of this brief glimpse into the life of the shepherds of the Picos de Europa.

WALK 6

El Mirador de Ordiales

Start/Finish	La Buferrera car park
Distance	23.6km
Ascent/Descent	1135m
Grade	Difficult
Time	7–8hr
Terrain	Good tracks and paths to Vegarredonda, then a good but rocky path.
Map	Editorial Alpina, 1:25,000. Picos de Europa, Macizo Occidental
Access	See 'Walks from La Buferrera' (Walk 2)
Route finding	The route follows the PR-PNPE 5 waymarked footpath throughout.

This is one of the classic walks of the Picos de Europa. It takes you to the tomb of Pedro Pidal, the founding father of the Spanish National Park system. From Ordiales you get breathtaking views in all directions – forwards, back, along, up and (especially) down. Easily done in a single day, there is a lot to recommend arriving at Ordiales in the afternoon, then spending the night at Vegarredonda prior to doing Walk 7 or 8.

Buferrera

CO-4

P
SF

Porra de Enol ▲

Lago Enol

Los Lagos de Covadonga

Lago Ercina

VEGA DE ENOL

Pandecarmen

P

Monte Palomberu woods

Río Pomperi

Vega la Piedra

Vega de Canrasu

Porru Llaguiellu ▲

Río Junjumía

Colláu Gamonal ✕

Vegarredonda 1410m ⌂

Cuenye Cerrada

Campos de Torga

Ordiales ▲

Pico Cotalba ▲

Mirador de Ordiales ✳

Sierra Cuenca ▲

Río Dobra

N

0   1
⊢━━━━┥ km

If you decide to leave your own car at Pandecarmen, park close to other vehicles so as to stop cows moving between cars and damaging mirrors and/or bodywork with their horns.

From the **Buferrera car park** (1040m) go up to the **Lago Enol** and follow PR-PNPE 5 round the N shore of the tarn to pick up a jeep track. Follow the track pleasantly across the **Vega de Enol** and enjoy the excellent views south to the Torre de Santa María and its neighbouring summits. The track ends at the small car park at **Pandecarmen** where parking is currently permitted even for private vehicles (3.5km; 1070m. Park information board). ◄ From the Pandecarmen car park follow the old mule trail down to a bridge across the river **Pomperi** at the site of the Pozo del Alemán (4.2km; 1060m).

> The *pozo* (pool) is named after the German-born romanticist **Roberto Frassinelli**, who often bathed there after a day in the Picos. Condemned in Germany for his liberal ideas, he emigrated to Spain in 1836. His interest in early church architecture eventually brought him to Asturias, where he married a woman from the nearby village of Corao. An accomplished draughtsman, Frassinelli, took part in drawing up the designs of the basilica in Covadonga (Walks 1 and 4).

Follow the now disused track up and across a sequence of fine mountain pastures; first **Vega la Piedra**, with the huge boulder that gives it its name, and then **Vega de Canrasu** (5.9km; 1230m), with its impressive views south to the north face of the Torre de Santa María. The track dwindles to a path and finally tops out at the **Colláu Gamonal** (7.8km; 1450m) which offers good views across to the **Vegarredonda huts**, both old and new. Follow the path down to the new hut (8.6km; 1410m).

> The new hut was built in the late 1980s as part of a highly contested plan to build large, **alpine-style huts** in numerous places in the Picos de Europa. The plan was abandoned early on because of the work of a local conservation group, the Colectivo Montañero por la Defensa de los Picos de Europa.

The architecture of the new Vegarredonda hut reflects that of the local shepherds' *majadas* in an attempt to mitigate its impact on their surroundings.

Follow the PR-PNPE 5 path from just behind the hut and go briefly SW, then W before zig-zagging SSW up a broad, rocky gully, the **Cuenye Cerrada**, to a col. Descend briefly and follow the path as it contours generally W below the northern slopes of the Pico Cotalba. ▶

At the end of the **Campos de Torga** traverse, follow the path as it swings S (10.6km; 1660m) and climbs briefly to enter the Vega de Ordiales. Climb up to the refuge in the middle of the *vega* (11.4km; 1702m) and then go on and up to the **Mirador de Ordiales** (11.8km; 1750m). This is the site of the tomb of Pedro Pidal, and it offers stunning views S and W to multiple summits in the Cordillera Cantábrica. For those with a good head for

Starting the traverse of the Campos de Torga

There are good views NW and N throughout this section, especially towards the Sueve range on the coast near Ribadesella.

heights, there are also thrilling views down to the Angón valley a 1000m below.

It was **Pedro Pidal's** express desire to have his body buried at Ordiales. His wishes were fulfilled in 1949 when numerous mountaineers took it in turns to carry his remains to what today is a fitting memorial to his work. A Senator in the Spanish parliament, he was the main force behind the creation of the Spanish National Park system at the beginning of the 20th century, and was the first person to climb El Naranjo de Bulnes, assisted by Gregorio Pérez, a shepherd from the village of Caín.

The tombstone at Ordiales reads: "Enamoured of the National Park of the Mountain of Covadonga, we would wish to live, die and rest eternally here, but the latter in Ordiales, in the magic world of the *rebecos* and eagles – there where we know the joy of the sky and the earth – there where we spent hours in admiration, emotion, dreams and transports of delight – there where we worshipped God in his work as the Supreme Craftsman – there where Nature appeared to us to be truly a temple."

Return along the same route.

There is a lot to be said for doing the first section of Walk 6 and then leaving unnecessary gear at the Vegarredonda hut before going on to the Mirador de Ordiales. If you then return to the Vegarredonda hut and spend the night there, the following morning you will be perfectly placed to attempt either Walk 7 or Walk 8. Staying at the hut before tackling either of these walks will be less demanding on your energies. With this in mind, the GPS track provided, together with the distances shown in the route description, start and end at the Vegarredonda hut.

WALK 7
Tour of the Torre de Santa María

Start/Finish	Vegarredonda hut (or the Buferrera car park; see Walk 6)
Distance	10.1km from Vegarredonda (27.3km from the Buferrera)
Ascent/Descent	1105m from Vegarredonda (1645m from the Buferrera)
Grade	Very difficult
Time	4–5hr from Vegarredonda (8–10hr from the Buferrera)
Terrain	Easy to the Colláu les Marines, then steadily wilder. The descent from the Jorcada de Santa María requires care.
Map	Editorial Alpina, 1:25,000. Picos de Europa, Macizo Occidental
Access	See 'Walks from La Buferrera', above.
Route finding	Easy except for the descent into the Jou Santu

This walk takes you up into some wild, remote, high-mountain terrain. On reaching the Jorcada de Santa María and sighting the difficulties of the descent into the desolate Jou Santu, the temptation to turn back is not insignificant. But neither are the rewards if you decide to go on, and the sense of achievement on looking back from the Boca del Jou Santu to the immense north wall of Peña Santa de Castilla (for information on the Peñas Santas, see Walk 3) makes it all worth the effort.

From the hut at **Vegarredonda** (0km; 1410m) head off SSE, up past the old climbers' hut, and on up towards the **Llampa Cimera**. Near the head of this broad gully, the path divides at a large cairn (1.8km; 1815m). Take the R fork and pass beneath the imposing **Porru Llobu** pinnacle, before following the old mule path as it zig-zags up to a shoulder just E of the **Colláu les Marines**, sometimes known as La Mazada (3.3km; 2108m). The views from the shoulder cover huge sections of the Cordillera Cantábrica to the SW and W, of the Dobra valley below and SW (Walk 9), and of the rock walls of the Torres de Cebolleda and the Torrezuela summits to the SE and S.

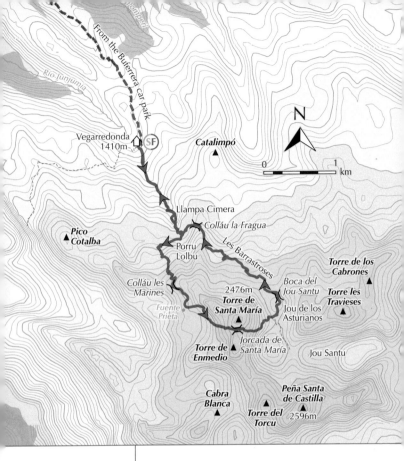

Cebolleda may be a reference to the heavily stratified rock visible in parts of the lower summit walls (cebolla = onion).

From the shoulder, follow the obvious track as it snakes around SW below the walls of the Torres de Cebolleda. ◄ **Fuente Prieta**, the last reliable water before getting back to Vegarredonda, will soon appear below the path to the right (3.7km; 2120m). Stay high and struggle up the vague, loose path that climbs to the the **Jorcada de Santa María** (4.8km; 2346m).

With care, descend E from the Jorcada de Santa María; the first section is slabby and slippery and has been the site of a number of accidents. When the terrain eases, swing round NE over slabby ground, staying close to the SW walls of the Torre de Santa María. It soon becomes necessary to follow tiny cairns E down the steep, broken ground that leads to the path clearly visible on the E side of the Jou Santu. Once on the path follow it N around the E side of the **Jou de los Asturianos** to a broad col, the **Boca del Jou Santu** (6.3km; 2090m), and the start of the descent back towards Vegarredonda. ▸

Go N from the col and then follow a good path as it works its way NW across **Les Barrastroses** down to the **Colláu la Fragua**, a tiny, grassy col below the N end of the Los Argaos ridge (8.1km; 1913m). Soon after this, the path enters the **Llampa Cimera** at the large cairn passed early on in the day. and it only remains to make your way down to the hut at **Vegarredonda** (10.1km; 1450m).

Take the chance to take one last look back at the huge, brooding N wall of Peña Santa de Castilla.

The new hut at Vegarredonda

WALK 8
Torre les Travieses

Start/Finish	Vegarredonda hut (or the Buferrera car park; see Walk 6)
Distance	10.9km from Vegarredonda (28km from the Buferrera car park)
Ascent/Descent	1010m from Vegarredonda (1550m from the Buferrera car park)
Grade	Very difficult
Time	4–5hr from Vegarredonda (8–10hr from the Buferrera car park)
Terrain	A good path most of the way, but some steep, trackless ground above the Jou de los Asturianos.
Map	Editorial Alpina, 1:25,000. Picos de Europa, Macizo Occidental
Access	See 'Walks from La Buferrera' (Walk 2)
Route finding	Straightforward to the Jou de los Asturianos. The section from there to the summit should not be undertaken in poor weather.

This is one of the more testing routes in this guide and the final section from the Jou de los Asturianos is not without certain difficulties, starting with gaining access to the col to the N of the Torre de los Asturianos. It is worth persevering, however; the summit views of Peña Santa de Castilla and the other summits surrounding the Jou Santu are stunning, and you need a good head for heights to be comfortable looking down to El Boquete and beyond. In short, a mountaineer's summit that is immensely rewarding on the right day.

From the hut at **Vegarredonda** (0km; 1410m) head off SSE up past the old climbers' hut, and on up towards the **Llampa Cimera**. Near the head of this broad gully, the path divides at a large cairn (1.8km; 1815m). Take the L fork and climb up NE and then E to the **Colláu la Fragua** (2.1km; 1913m). From La Fragua start the long

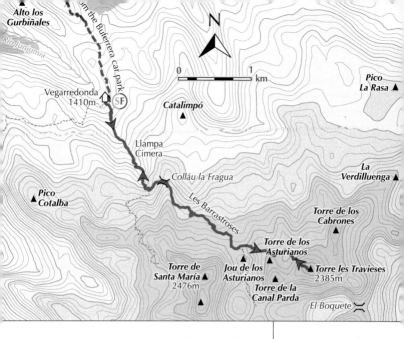

rising traverse of **Les Barrastroses**. This well-made path climbs steadily up below the imposing N walls of the Torre de Santa María with only occasional brief descents. Eventually the path swings S and skirts round the SW side of Pt 2133 to reach the **Jou de los Asturianos** (4km; 2090m), with the north wall of Peña Santa de Castilla brooding menacingly over the whole scene to the S.

From the point of arrival at the Jou de los Asturianos make a rising trackless traverse to gain the col that lies between Pt 2133 and the **Torre de los Asturianos**. There is a very short section of simple scrambling as you do this. Now follow the many small cairns that climb up to and then skirt E around the base of the Torre de los Asturianos, then drop down NE slightly to the slabby, heavily eroded ground to the N of the deep Jou de la Canal Parda. ▶

Head ENE on slabby ground staying N of the Jou de la Canal Parda until the cairns invite you to swing SE (approx. 4.8km; 2200m) and head up the broad N spur of the **Torre les Travieses**. A short, loose gully gives access to

Provided you don't get lost, this section of the route gives you an opportunity to study the effects of karstification and water erosion on limestone at close quarters.

The old Vegarredonda hut and the Llampa Cimera

the upper reaches of the spur, and a final shallow, grassy gully comes out at the col just W of the summit (5.4km; 2385m). A solar panel, radio antenna and the box of an emergency transmitter for use by the rescue services are located on the summit.

The best summits for getting the feel of an area are not always the highest, and the **Torre les Travieses** is a case in point. All the summits to the S and W are higher, including the Torre de Santa María (2476m) and imposing Peña Santa de Castilla (2596m). But few other summits give you such a privileged view of the Jou Santu, whose stark wildness seems to be further heightened by the act of peering down into it from Les Travieses. Anyone with a head for heights will thoroughly enjoy locating El Boquete, for example, the col that connects the Jou Santu to the tiny village of Caín, over 1500m below.

Descend by the same route.

WALK 9
La Jocica and La Senda del Arcediano

Start/Finish	Collada de Angón, Amieva
Distance	22km
Ascent/Descent	1120m
Grade	Difficult
Time	7–8hr
Terrain	Old tracks and paths. The Senda del Arcediano is tricky in places.
Map	Editorial Alpina, 1:25,000. Picos de Europa, Macizo Occidental
Access	Head S from Cangas de Onís on the N-625. At Ceneya take the minor road E up to Amieva. Just before reaching the village a concrete track goes off E past the cemetery. Follow this through woodland to a junction. Turn R and continue up to the Collada de Angón, a small car park and various information boards.
Route finding	Straightforward except for a short section after El Chamozo.

Without taking in a single summit, this circular route takes you through lush fields and meadows and then up into some spectacular middle-mountain terrain. The first part of the route follows the upper reaches of the Dobra river and offers a bird's-eye view of the Jocica Gorge and Dam. The central part of the walk takes you into high pastures and through ancient beech forests. The descent follows a centuries-old drove road, the Senda del Arcediano, parts of which have been cobbled since Medieval times.

Start at the **Collada de Angón** (815m) and descend steeply on a concrete track into the lushness of the Valle

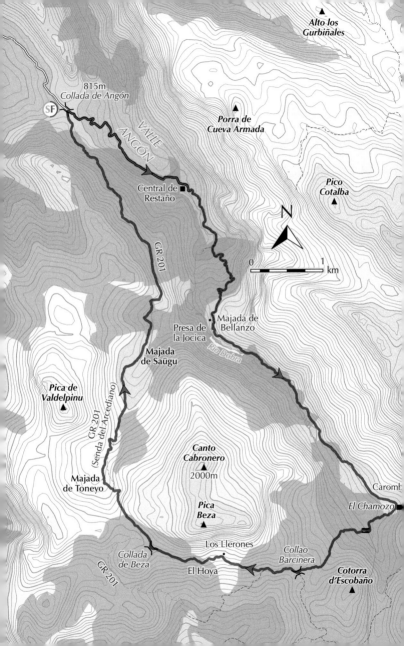

The Central del Restaño seen from the Mirador de Ordiales (Walk 6)

de Angón. The concrete comes to an end at the **Central del Restaño** (2.5km; 720m). ▸

Cross the **River Dobra** and climb up along the R bank under the shadow of the huge walls that hem the **Angón valley** into the N and E. As you climb higher, the hazels that have lined much of the route so far begin to give way to beech, then the track steepens and snakes steeply up to the **Majada de Bellanzo**. Here it levels off and soon after you reach the site of the **Presa de la Jocica** (6km; 990m). Follow the stairs down to a small platform for excellent views of the dam and the gorge.

The **Jocica Dam** was built between 1959 and 1963, the materials needed being brought up in 4WD vehicles along the track you followed to this point. The waters of the dam still drive the turbines in Restaño power plant below and, although the idea

The Central de Restaño is one of a number of small hydroelectric power stations that have made use of the Picos' water resources since the early 20th century.

of building a dam in a place like the Jocica Gorge is unthinkable today, it was seen very much as forward-thinking in its day. This was clean energy long before we even began to use the term or worry about where our energy was coming from.

A narrow path leads away from the Jocica dam in exposed positions. Follow the path along the bank of the Dobra, first in open ground and then in woodland. It is easy to lose the best path here. Eventually the trees give way to open slopes (7.8km; approx. 1000m) and, soon after, you come to the high pastures of **Carombo**. These

The Presa de la Jocica

are dominated to the E by the walls of the Western Massif, and to the W by those of Peña Beza (Walk 34) and the Canto Cabronero. On the far side of Carombo there is a lone cabin, **El Chamozo** (9.6km; 1120m), and a spring with excellent water.

From the cabin descend to the river (poor waymarking), and cross the Dobra on a small bridge, the Puente de Carombo (10.2km; 1050m). A long haul up through superb mature beech woods comes out at the **Collao Barcinera** (11.7km; 1331m). Here a track descends S to Vegabaño, some 15 minutes away. Ignore this and strike off W on a track signposted PR-PNPE 7 Beza-Soto. After a few minutes branch off R again onto a narrow path (12.12km; 1350m). This traverses below the walls of Peña Beza and, after negotiating **Los Llerones**, a labyrinth of gigantic blocks where it is easy to get off the best path, you come out at **El Hoya** (13.2km; 1450m). ▸

From El Hoya skirt round below Peña Beza to the **Collada de Beza** (14.1km; 1511m). The waymarking is poor on this col, but the correct route climbs very gently N to a gate, the Portilla del Tarabicu, where you join the **Senda del Arcediano** (GR 201) which has come in from the L from Soto de Sajambre.

El Hoya offers fabulous views down to the jewel of Soto de Sajambre, across to the summits of the Cordillera Cantábrica, S to the Pico Jario above Vegabaño, and back E to the Torre Bermeja on the southern edge of the Western Massif of the Picos.

The **Senda del Arcediano** would originally have been a Roman road, though the first documented evidence of the drove road dates from the 10th century. The current name, however, comes from the 17th century, when Pedro Díaz de Oseja, the Archdeacon of Villaviciosa in Asturias, left money in his will for the upkeep of the trail. Drove roads such as this were vital to life on either side of the mountains. Salt, fish and wood were transported from the coast to the interior, and wine and wheat brought back. Until the construction of the modern road, the N625 from the Puerto del Pontón to Cangas de Onís, all of these goods would have used the Senda del Arcediano.

The Majada de Toneyo and the Pica de Valdelpinu

The route back to Amieva follows the Senda del Arcediano. Start by descending steeply into the **Majada de Toneyo** (15.4km; 1350m). The Majada de Toneyo lies off the path to the L but is well worth visiting. It not only contains the remains of old shepherds' huts, but also of cubiles, circular stone constructions where pigs would have been kept.

Some parts of the lower section of the Arcediano are still rough cobbled in much the same way they would have been in Roman times.

From Toneyo descend comfortably to **Majada de Saügu** (17.3km; 1150m), cross scrubby ground, and come out quite suddenly in superb situations above the whole of the Angón valley (18.6km; 1140m). The Jocica Gorge is visible off R, and the River Dobra passes dizzily by hundreds of metres below. It only now remains to follow the Senda del Arcediano back to the **Collada de Angón** (22km), and the end of a great day. ◀

CABRALES

El Naranjo de Bulnes and the Pico de Albo from Vanu (Walk 12)

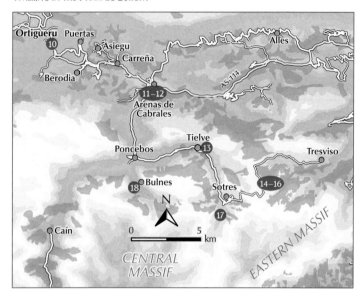

The walks in the Cabrales sector lie in the northern reaches of the Eastern and Central massifs. Unlike those in the Onís sector, many walks in Cabrales involve considerable height gain and loss, as well as long sections of rough, sometimes trackless, high-mountain terrain. Despite this, the draw of the sector is irresistible – the spectacular Cares Gorge, Bulnes, the tiny village I passed through on my first visit to the Picos, and El Naranjo de Bulnes, or Picu Urriellu as it is known today, the king of the Picos skies, the mountain that left me speechless back in 1979.

The main town, Arenas de Cabrales, is conveniently situated at the entrance to the Cares Gorge. This makes it a major gateway for walking in the Central and Eastern Massifs, and for access to delightful mountain villages such as Tielve, Sotres or Tresviso. Arenas and the nearby district capital, Carreña, offer most of the services you are likely to need – banks, supermarkets, shops, equipment stores, bars, restaurants and simple tourist information services. As is the case everywhere in the Picos, a wide range of accommodation is available, as well as a good campsite 2km east of Arenas.

The Cabrales district is famous for its unique blue cheese, and a visit to a show cave is well worth an hour of anyone's time. Equally strong are the ties the district has with El Naranjo de Bulnes (Picu Urriellu). The best

At Silla del Caballo col (Walk 15)

viewpoints for this iconic mountain are at the Mirador del Pozo de la Oración, on the road between Arenas and Carreña; the Mirador Pedro Udaondo, which lies a short distance ENE of the village of Asiegu, and Camarmeña, the tiny hamlet immediately above Poncebos.

The village of Bulnes is a major tourist spot and can be accessed on foot up the impressive Canal del Tejo, as it has been for centuries, or by the modern funicular railway. Both routes start in Poncebos, the busy hamlet at the northern end of the Cares Gorge. You can reserve tickets for the railway at: www.alsa.com/en/web/bus/regional/asturias/bulnes-funicular.

During the peak summer months access to Poncebos is regulated by the national park wardens because of the limited parking space. However, this does not stop you from going through Poncebos and on up to Tielve or Sotres. If stopped, just make your final destination clear to the warden. In 2022 a new bus service ran to Poncebos from the main car park in Arenas, with a connecting service from Poncebos up to Tielve and Sotres.

An infrequent but regular bus service links Arenas to Cangas de Onís via Carreña, Ortigueru and Benia. For details, see www.alsa.com/en/web/bus/home. There is also an infrequent service to Panes, the entry to the Liébana valley. Taxis can be found easily in both Arenas and Poncebos. For telephone numbers see https://www.cabrales.es/taxis.

WALK 10
Pueblos de Cabrales

Start	Ortigueru
Finish	Carreña
Distance	10.7km
Ascent	345m
Descent	575m
Grade	Moderate
Time	4hr
Terrain	Tracks and good minor roads. A little uneven over the central section.
Map	Adrados Ediciones, 1:50,000. Parque Nacional de los Picos de Europa
Access	From Carreña take a taxi or the local bus to Casa Manolo in Ortigueru
Route finding	Not difficult except for a short section after Puertas.

The Picos de Europa are as much about villages as they are about summits. Using minor roads and old farm tracks, this ambling walk links five villages in the Cabrales district. The villages all lie amid lush middle-mountain pastures and offer increasingly good views of the Central Massif, with the second half of the walk dominated almost entirely by El Naranjo de Bulnes. An excellent walk for an easier day or for a family outing.

From Casa Manolo (400m) walk NW 50m, cross the **AS-114** road and swing S on a lane that winds its way through the main section of the Ortigueru. Come out at the main road (0.45km), cross this, and take the minor road signed off L to Pandiellu and Puertas.

Walk past the church and cemetery and then follow the road, first E and then NE, to a high point above Pandiellu (2km; 490m) with good views E and SE over the Cabrales district, and then beyond the northern reaches of the Eastern and Central Massifs. ◄

There are lovely views back to Ortigueru over this section of the walk.

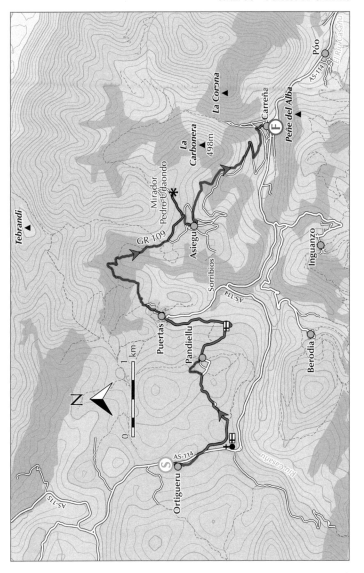

*Ortigueru from
the first section
of the walk*

Turn L on a jeep track and climb briefly before descending into **Pandiellu**. Wander down to the last of the houses on the E side of the village and re-join the road from Ortigueru. Follow this down until it curves round the ruins of a church after offering a bird's eye view of the village **cemetery** (3.2km; 390m).

As in the UK, burials in Spain originally took place in sacred ground in and around the church. In the late 18th century this practice was declared insanitary. The foul air and real risk of plague and disease was enough for King Carlos III to order cemeteries to be built well away from churches and villages. Although the measure was unpopular, by the middle of the 19th century all towns and villages in Spain had a **cemetery** built at what was felt to be a safe distance from the village itself. This is the case with all the villages of the Picos de Europa.

From the cemetery, follow the road N amid fields and enter **Puertas** (4.1km; 340m). After wandering around the village, locate Villa María in the main square. Head up quite steeply E from Villa María, and work on up through the village to its NE corner.

> As with many villages in and around the Picos, Puertas benefitted from the return of immigrants at the beginning of the 20th century. **Los Indianos**, as the returning immigrants were known, had made their fortunes in the Americas and invested their money where they had been born. Villa María is a small but classic Indianos house.

Some 100m after the last of the houses, go L at a junction on a concreted track. This begins to climb quite steeply and El Naranjo de Bulnes comes into view for the first time on the R across the valley. Follow the lane to where it tops out and swings NW (5km; 420m). Drop down R on a narrow track with **GR 109** signposting for Carreña. The little-used track contours around above the Río de Ricao valley, then drops steeply down to cross the stream before climbing up to the outskirts of **Asiegu** (6.7km; 450m). ▶ Contour round SE above the rooftops of Asiegu until it is possible to go off NE and walk up steeply to the **Mirador Pedro Udaondo** picnic area (7.4km; 480m).

There are good views back to Puertas at this point, but what draws the eye again and again is El Naranjo de Bulnes to the SSE.

> The picnic area has excellent views south to El Naranjo de Bulnes and its neighbouring peaks. The light is especially good in the afternoon, when the sun comes onto the great west face of this iconic mountain. There is a memorial plaque to **Pedro Udaondo**, a Basque mountaineer who dedicated a large part of his climbing career to the Picos de Europa. A number of classic problems of the 1950s were resolved by Udaondo's skilled hands, including the first winter ascent of El Naranjo. Udaondo was killed in the Picos in 2007 when he slipped during a winter climb in the Western Massif. He was 73 when he fell.

Having soaked up the views, return to the previous junction, cross the road and descend into **Asiegu**. As with the other villages in this walk, take time to absorb the atmosphere and become acquainted with the traditional architectural styles.

Every year the international Premios Princesa de Asturias chooses an exemplary village in Asturias. In 2019, the village chosen was **Asiegu** because of the way it had maintained its traditions, especially those related to cheese-making, whilst adapting to the challenges of modern times.

Leave the village going down past the church and then the covered sports facility. Turn E along the road but almost immediately take a track that descends off R and enters woodland. When the track comes out on the road from Asiegu to Carreña (9.6km; 280m), follow this down round a hairpin, and then take a track off L and SE towards Carreña. Cross a stile to enter a field (10.2km; 225m). Leave the field by a second stile and enter **Carreña** next to a modern house. Amble down through the town, the capital of the Cabrales district, to come out at Casa Coro (10.7km; 220m), an excellent spot to relax and enjoy the remains of the day.

WALK 11
Cabeza de Juanrobre

Start/Finish	Riverside car park in Arenas de Cabrales
Distance	11.4km
Ascent/Descent	800m
Grade	Moderate
Time	5–6hr
Terrain	A good track over the first third. A rocky, slippery central section. A good path on descent.
Map	Editorial Alpina, 1:25,000. Picos de Europa, Macizo Central y Oriental
Access	Along the AS-114 from Cangas de Onís or Panes. The car park lies immediately S of the river Cares.
Route finding	Not difficult except for one short section.

The view E from Arenas de Cabrales is dominated by the rocky summits of the Cabeza Cerréu and the higher Cabeza de Juanrobre. This walk follows an old livestock trail to the Invernales de Nava and offers excellent views from the Cabeza de Juanrobre, both of Arenas and of the summits of the high Picos de Europa. This shorter walk is a great option when poor weather means the higher routes are out of bounds.

Leave the **car park** (0km; 145m) heading E over a wooden bridge. Go up a narrow lane to the main road and cross this diagonally R to gain another lane between old houses. This leads to a square and the Capilla de San Juan. Follow the road as it swings N past the new care home and then the town's health centre. Turn E just after this and follow a tarmac road past the **Vega de Tordín cheesery**. ▶

Just after you cross a stream, take the track that goes off L (1.1km; 145m) and follow this up to where the concrete surface ends and a livestock trail continues amid hazel and ash scrub. After swinging back L the trail ends,

The guided tour of the cheesery is well worth the time it takes if you want know more about the excellent Cabrales cheese, which is traditionally made from a mixture of cow, sheep and goats' milk. There is a small shop, too.

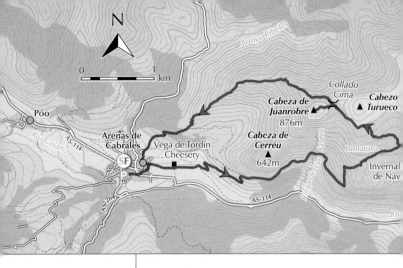

and a path cuts off R (2km; 255m), goes past a cabin and then quickly picks up a good trail coming in from the L.

The River Cares from the path up to the Invernales de Nava

After going through a rudimentary gate (2.2km), the well-worn trail comes out into open ground and offers good views down along the spectacular gorge cut by the River Cares. Perfectly graded, the trail climbs gently E and then NE below the Cabeza de Cerréu (642m) until it reaches the **Riega de Vau Azares**, which in rainy weather is a full-blown waterfall.

The trail continues to climb, first SE, then due N and finally E as it passes a good spring and enters the pastures of the **Invernales de Nava** (4.4km; 610m) and the trail becomes a simple path across the meadows to a second spring, the **Fuente la Batuva** (4.9km; 685m), which is hidden among trees in the N corner of the meadows. ▶

From above the Batuva spring head up ENE on a narrow path until this suddenly swings N (5.3km; 735m) and drops down into muddy, uncomfortable rocky ground amid bushes. The path passes next to an abandoned hut; this is the worst section of the walk and it is important to continually locate the red paint dots that mark out the route. The discomfort eases as more open ground is reached (6km; 750m) and this is followed via the regular red point dots as the path contours round the SW slopes of the **Cabezo Turueco** to the Collado Cima (6.7km; 801m), where bags can be left before the assault on the summit of the **Cabeza de Juanrobre** (7km; 876m). In clear weather the views here are outstanding, and not only of the three massifs of the Picos de Europa.

After descending from the summit and collecting your bag, head NW down and around the N slopes of the Juanrobre summit. You will reach a shoulder to the N of the summit and the rock type changes suddenly to dark, sandy quartzite. A long spur lies below, dropping down W and then SW to **Arenas**. A narrow but comfortable path descends the spur amid heather and some broom lower down, staying mostly just down L of the ridge itself.

The Picos de Europa are one of the **major limestone ranges** in Europe, but limestone is not the only rock to be found here. During the Alpine Orogeny, some 50 million years ago, the fracturing and thrusting

The Spanish for winter is invierno. Invernales are grazing areas where livestock can be kept when they are brought down from summer pastures.

of the deep layers of sedimentary rocks in the area drove the limestone and sandstone beds upwards so that they were left sloping down towards the north and laid one on top of the other like a deck of cards at an angle. In the process the sandstone became transformed into quartzite, a much harder rock.

Layers of quartzite appear in numerous places along the northern edge of the Picos de Europa (Walk 1), and the descent of Walk 11 follows a tilted band of quartzite. Under foot the rock is clearly darker, although in many ways it feels and looks like sandstone. The vegetation is also quite different – quartzite creates acid soils and this gives rise to heathers and broom as opposed to the brackens and grass of limestone soils. The change in the shape of the land and in the vegetation is quite marked over the second part of the Walk 11 when compared to the first.

WALK 12

El Cuetón

Start	Arenas de Cabrales car park
Finish	Poncebos
Distance	18.4km
Ascent	1540m
Descent	1475m
Grade	Very difficult
Time	8–10hr
Terrain	The ascent uses well-trodden livestock tracks and paths. These are steep and exposed in places. The highest ground is trackless. The descent is continually steep and the path is very vague over one short section.
Map	Editorial Alpina, 1:25,000. Picos de Europa, Macizo Central y Oriental
Access	The Arenas car park lies just S of the river. A summer bus service and taxis connect Poncebos to the car park.
Route finding	Not difficult, except for one part of the descent.

El Cuetón is the more common name for what the Alpina map calls the Cabeza de las Esmeradas. Whatever the name, this unobtrusive summit is a stunning viewpoint for places in and around Arenas de Cabrales, and an outstanding one for El Naranjo de Bulnes and the Cares Gorge. The price to pay for these views is the huge height gain and subsequent loss, the descent to Poncebos being very steep almost throughout. But for those willing to make the effort, for good or for bad this traverse makes for an unforgettable day.

Walk out of the **car park**, going past the taxi stand and Poncebos bus stop. Turn L on the road to Poncebos, and just before this goes over the River Cares, strike off R (signed 'Invernales de Vanu'). The track makes its way up amid ancient, coppiced chestnut trees, and initially offers good views back to Arenas and the Cabeza de Juanrobre beyond (Walk 11).

As the track climbs it yields unusual views of the Cares Gorge and the summits of the Torrecerredo group. At a junction (2km; 345m), take the L fork. El Naranjo de Bulnes soon comes into view, and not long after the woods recede and the track comes out at a well-used jeep track between walled fields. The jeep track meets a road 200m further on, with a small picnic area off to the R (2.6km; 410m). This is Vanu and offers excellent views of El Naranjo de Bulnes, the first of the day.

Turn L onto the road, which quickly becomes a good track entering woodland heading W. At a junction with another track, go L and continue to climb, crossing a cattle grid, then coming out at a hut with a spring and drinking trough (4.3km; 585m). Stay on the track and climb up to a broad col with excellent views down to Inguanzo, and a junction with a good track coming up from this delightful village (4.9km; 640m).

We are so used to living wherever we want that we forget that valley bottoms used to be inhospitable places. The **villages** of Inguanzo, Berodia, Asiegu, Puertas and Pandiellu all occupy positions well above the valley bottom, and mostly on south-facing slopes.

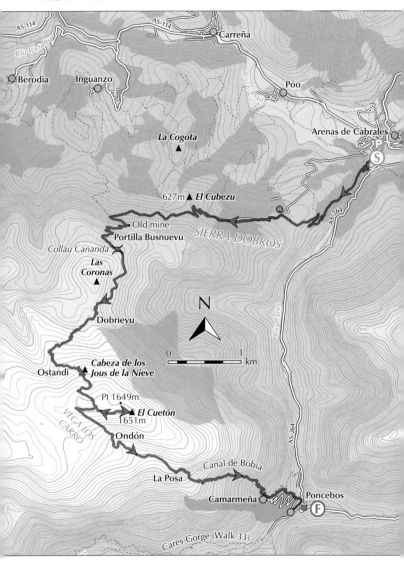

Inguanzo from below the Sierra Dobros

Follow the track as it rises steadily W across the northern slopes of the **Sierra Dobros**. After a sharp hairpin bend to the L (5.8km; 715m) follow the track steeply to where it ends at the entrance to an **old mine** (6.1km; 780m). A good path goes off R from the old mine entrance and climbs in exposed positions up to a gash in the Sierra Dobros rock walls. A wooden gate, the **Portilla Busnuevu** (6.8km; 930m), keeps livestock from venturing up or down the path at will. ▶

Go through the gate, climb briefly W, then work back SE and up to the **Colláu Cananda** (7.3km; 1017m), which yields wonderful views down the Cananda valley to the road from Arenas to Poncebos, and across E to the craggy outline of Portudera.

Drop down slightly and traverse S on a good path below the summit of **Las Coronas**. At the ruined huts at **Dobrieyu** (8.6km; 1150m) follow the path as it climbs

These paths have been used for centuries to take livestock up to summer pastures. Whole families would go up to the high pastures and live there all summer.

99

SW away from Dobrieyu. The path swings S and then E and enters **Ostandi**, with its cabins and small pond. Climb SE from here on an old livestock track and gain the col to the SW of the **Cabeza de los Joos de la Nieve** (10.7km; 1500m).

Stay on the grassy track which leads to a fenced, plastic water deposit. Follow the remains of the track as it climbs SE to a col with sudden, good views of El Naranjo de Bulnes (11.5km; 1610m). Still heading SE, cross rockier ground and then skirt around the S side of a deepish sink hole (*jou*) to gain the ridge that runs E–W in airy positions above the tiny cabins of Ondón and the depths of the Cares Gorge way below. Follow the airy ridge E to the summit of **El Cuetón**, the Cabeza de las Esmeradas on the Alpina map (12.1km; 1651m).

> Once on the **summit**, the exertions of the morning are immediately forgotten. The reward is a 360° panorama that starts to the N with the Sierra de Cuera, with the Cantabrian Sea beyond that to the NW. Most of the summits of the Western Massif are visible to the SW, dominated by the immense bulk of Peña Santa de Castilla. The Cares Gorge lies unnervingly at your feet, whilst to the S you seem to be but a stone's throw from the summits of the Central Massif, especially those from Peña Castil to the SE through to the Torrecerredo group due S. With a handful of summits visible in the Eastern Massif, it is obvious that this humble peak is a wonderful place to while away an hour or more soaking up the atmosphere and the views.

There are two options at this stage. One is to return to the start by the route you came up. The other, far more interesting option is to complete the full traverse by descending to Poncebos via the Majada de Ondón. To do this, retrace your steps until you have skirted back round the deepish sink hole. Abandon the ascent route at this point and head W so as to contour round the S slopes of **Pt 1649** and reach the broad grassy col of the **Vega los**

Carro (13km; 1580m). Swing left to head ESE and follow the animal paths that lead down with occasional cairns to the top of a steep, grassy, uninviting gully (13.5km; 1495m). Avoid this by breaking out R and descending on the vaguest of paths first ESE and then S, picking your way down the easiest ground on a poorly defined grassy rake with rocky ground both above and below. ▶

Take care over this section, which is exposed and needs a keen eye to find the easiest route.

This descent, which some will find intimidating, is a standard day for livestock coming over from Inguanzo to graze at Ondón. Their hooves leave mud stains on the pale limestone rock and churn up the grass. This can help you to spot the best route.

When you reach a grassy runnel, follow this SE to where the path swings N and drops down to another, larger grass runnel (13.9km; 1360m). This also leads SE and ends at a grass platform just below the cabins of **Ondón** (14.4km; 1280m). The platform offers outstanding views across the Cares Gorge to the Central Massif and is a good place to relax after the rigours of the last section of descent.

From the platform, follow the path comfortably down to the obvious grassy shoulder of **La Posa** (15km; 1230m),

El Naranjo de Bulnes from the Majada de Ondón

which offers excellent views of the Cares Gorge almost vertically below. After La Posa the path enters the **Canal de Bobia**. This is steep in places, and very steep elsewhere, and at times a little loose under foot. But again, the thought that livestock still make light work of this descent will prick your pride and keep you going.

After starting right up against the Paredines de la Bobia rock walls, the path works its way across to the R side of the huge Bobia gully. Later, shortly after passing a lone, ruined cabin (16km; 935m), it crosses L and brushes up once more against the huge containing rock walls, before going off R again to enter **Camarmeña** (17.2km; 480m).

If you have timed your day right, the agony of the seemingly endless descent down the Canal de Bobia will be cushioned by the spectacle of the afternoon sun on the west face of El Naranjo de Bulnes. This is one of the most iconic images of Spanish alpine climbing.

Follow the road steeply down through the Camarmeña to a junction (18.4km; 440m). Take the L fork (signed PR-PNPE 31 to Poncebos) and go past Casa Lobeto. Take the waymarked footpath over the huge pipes that carry water from the Cares down to the power station below. At a junction drop down R to come out at the road from Carmarmeña to Poncebos at a tight hairpin. Just below the hairpin descend to a concrete track. Take this and go down R to the bars and restaurants in **Poncebos**, where it is easy to find refreshment, a bus or taxi back to Arenas.

WALK 13
Monte Camba

Start/Finish	Tielve
Distance	13.5km
Ascent/Descent	750m
Grade	Moderate
Time	5–6hr
Terrain	Good paths and tracks. The old road from to Tielve is exposed in places.
Map	Editorial Alpina, 1:25,000. Picos de Europa, Macizo Central y Oriental
Access	Follow the CA-1 from Poncebos to Tielve. Drive up into the village proper (steep and narrow) and park in the village square.
Route finding	Care is needed on leaving Tobaos.

This official waymarked footpath, PR-PNPE 20, is much better than it looks on paper. The route takes you up to the *majadas* that serve Tielve even today, and in doing so provides you with little-seen views of the summits of the NE sector of the Central Massif, particularly Peña Maín and El Naranjo de Bulnes. The bird's-eye views of Sotres are also memorable, and the village is an excellent place to stop and re-charge your batteries before the spectacular descent back to Tielve along the old, cobbled drove road.

Climb steeply E out of the square past the washing sheds and a good spring. On reaching the village water deposit (0.3km; 747m), abandon the track and follow a path signposted Sotres. The path goes up through coppiced hazel and offers good views up the Duje valley and beyond to the Pico Boru in the Eastern Massif.

> The paths leading away from villages in many parts of the Picos are thickly lined by heavily **coppiced hazel bushes**. For centuries hazel has made

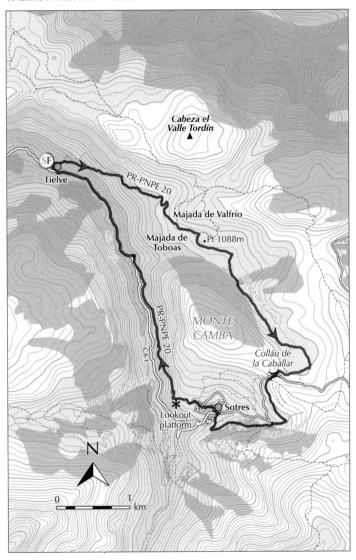

an important contribution to the rural economy throughout Northern Spain. The highly nutritious nuts are the most obvious product, but the leaves around the nuts were also of value, as they were used as bedding for the livestock during the winter. Coppicing the trees produced firewood from the older branches, and the strong, straight branches that grew back were ideal for weaving baskets. The thicker branches were greatly prized by shepherds to make the walking sticks without which they never ventured into the mountains. Hazel was also good at stabilizing the land where it was steep, or where riverbanks were threatened by flood waters.

A small shoulder provides excellent views back to Tielve basking in the sun, and not long after you'll join the main track (1.2km; 920m) at a spring. Turn R and climb up beyond the tree line to gain further good views back to Tielve, then continue climbing until you reach the cabins of the **Majada de Valfrío** (1.8km; 1000m). This is soon followed by the **Majada de Tobaos** (2.2km; 1045m), from where you can enjoy an unusual view of Peña Castil (Walk 17) and El Naranjo de Bulnes (Walk 18) in the Central Massif.

From a shoulder just beyond Tobaos follow the path down, taking care with route finding when you reach the tiny, muddy Riega de Cimbraña (2.8km; 1050m). Do not continue E. Instead, cross the stream and work S and then ESE around the slopes of Pt 1088. The path eventually enters the heavily wooded **Riega de Camba** ravine (Riega de la Caballar on the Boulan map / 3.9km; 1020m).

Work steadily up through the beech woods until the path comes out into open grazing land. Follow the path first S and then up W to the communications antennae and the many fine shepherds' huts at the **Colláu de la Caballar** (6.2km; 1235m). Cross the road and join the track to Sotres by the monument to the Vuelta Ciclista.

The Picos de Europa is regularly the scene of one of the stages in the **Vuelta de España**. Normally the

Walkers heading down to Tielve from Sotres just after crossing the Riega de Camba

The old road to Tielve proves delightful and you derive a certain sense of superiority as lesser beings speed past you in their cars lower down on the tarmac update.

gruelling ascent from Covadonga to the Lago de Ercina is chosen to end the Picos stage, but in 2015 the equally demanding end of 15th stage was from Poncebos to the Colláu de la Caballar.

Follow the track down enjoying the superb views of **Sotres** and Peña Maín before coming out in the village right next to Casa Cipriano, an excellent place to take on food and refreshment (8.5km; 1020m). Leave Sotres by climbing up to the very highest houses and the church. A good track leads W from just below the last house and goes past a **lookout platform** with picnic tables and an excellent view of the Upper Duje valley (9km; 1055m). Just after this, the track swings suddenly N and yields spectacular views down the Middle Duje valley towards Tielve. ◄

Eventually the old road merges with the new one and forces you back to reality (11.6km; 765m) and onto the tarmac. The next 2km to Tielve follow the new road, so take care with the traffic as you stroll down to the end of a straightforward but intriguing glimpse at the lives of two key Picos villages.

CABRALES CHEESE

If any two villages are associated with Cabrales cheese in the minds of people who know this part of the Picos de Europa, it is Sotres and Tielve. True, the Consejo Regulador, the cheese's governing body, has its offices in Carreña, but for many, Sotres and Tielve are the spiritual home of Cabrales cheese. As with the Gamonedo and Tresviso Picón cheeses, Cabrales is made from a mixture of sheep, goat and cow's milk, and in times past was matured in caves close to where it was made. The cheese is widely available in both villages, and if it has the seal of approval of the Consejo Regulador, it will come wrapped in dark green, aluminium foil.

WALK 14
Vao los Llobos

Start/Finish	Joyu el Teju car park (1300m)
Distance	15.5km
Ascent/Descent	700m
Grade	Moderate
Time	5–6hr
Terrain	Good tracks and paths throughout.
Map	Editorial Alpina, 1:25,000. Picos de Europa, Macizo Central y Oriental
Access	Take the AS-264 from Arenas de Cabrales to Poncebos, then the CA-1 to Sotres. Drive E up and out of Sotres, over the Colláu de la Caballar and on to the car park on the E side of the Joyu el Teju.
Route finding	Easy, following PR-PNPE 28 almost throughout.

This is another route proving that an excellent mountain day is not only about reaching summits. It's also a great opportunity to enjoy the immense beauty of the beech woods that clothe so much of the Picos middle mountain. In addition, the visit to the Casetón de Ándara is a chance to get close to the mining industry that fashioned so many places in the Eastern Massif, and that was responsible for the tracks followed on this walk from start to finish.

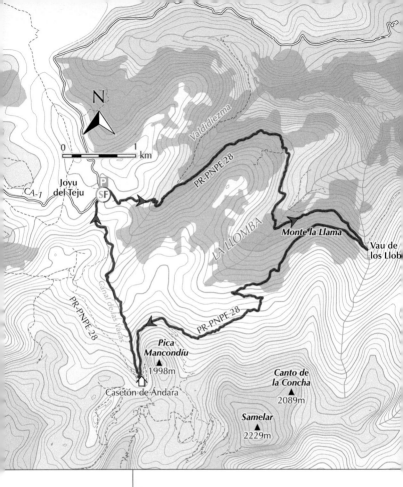

These woods are a delight if caught early in the morning with the sun filtering down through the leaves and the mountain air still cool.

Leave the Joyu del Teju car park at the information board and head E. The track descends quite steeply at first and then levels out on reaching the Valdidiezma woods (1.5km; 1090m). ◄

Continue through the woods at an appropriately relaxed pace until the trees finally recede and the track comes out into open land (4km; 1060m). Go round La Llomba, the long grassy spur that comes down from the R.

Llomba is an Asturian word referring to long mountain spur. In the Picos many of these are the result of lateral glacial moraines. In the upper part of the Duje valley, for example, the track from Sotres to Áliva goes up the spur known as the Llomba del Toro (Bull's Spur). The base of La Llomba on this walk gives you your first glimpse of the Pica Mancondíu far above to the SW.

Follow the track comfortably to where it re-enters the beech woods, which are now part of the **Monte la Llama**. There are good views down left over this section to the cabins of El Cerezal and across to the village of Tresviso, which clings uncomfortably to the side of the Sierra Cocón. Shortly after the track comes back out of the woods you come to the junction and the drinking trough at **Vao de los Lobos** (6.5km; 1130m). Turn sharp

Pico Mancondíu on rounding La Llomba

R here and double back on yourself as you to start the climb up through beech woods towards the summit walls of the **Pica Macondíu**.

Follow the track out of the woods (9km; 1340m) to get a head-on view of the Mancondíu, which now seems to tower above you. Once out of the woods and into the sun, the track will feel steeper than it is. On a hot day you will suffer as you zig-zag up, but if you do, spare a thought for the miners who had to use this route on a daily basis.

MINING IN THE EASTERN MASSIF

The tracks in this part of the Eastern Massif were all built to facilitate the **mining operations** that brought lead and zinc out of the Picos de Europa. Mining began in 1859 with the work of the Minas de la Providencia, and continued until the second half of the 20th century. These were deep mines and the minerals brought out, galena and zinc blend, had to be taken down for treatment at the Hornos (ovens) del Dobrillo just above Beges. The treated materials were then carried to La Hermida, where boats were used to take them down the River Deva and to Unquera for shipping abroad.

The middle section of this walk coincides with the track from La Hermida to Ándara, which covered a distance of 15km and overcame a height difference of 1700m. This is no small achievement and, although the mining industry has had a number of undesirable impacts on the landscape of the Picos de Europa, the miners' tracks have eased access to many parts of the range. Moreover, it is a mark of the skill of those who built these tracks for ox carts in the 19th century, that 4WD vehicles can still use many of them today if required to do so.

Follow the track to a junction just below the Mancondíu (11.2km; 1640m). It does not matter which fork you take; either option will lead you to the **Casetón de Ándara** (12.5km; 1725m), but the R option means less work and offers splendid views of the coast, and an equally surprising view of the mine workings at the head of the Canal de las Vacas. The hut lies just above the main track to the L and is one of the smallest in the Picos de Europa. A possible base for Walks 17 and 18, on

The Andara hut with the PR-PNPE 28 descent track visible off left

this walk the hut will provide refreshment and welcome respite from the sun on a hot day. There is a spring of cool drinking water just below it. ▶

From the hut the PR-PNPE 28 follows the miners' track NNW back to the Joyu el Teju car park, but ignore this and instead drop down into the **Canal de las Vacas**. As the name suggests (*vaca* = cow), this was the way live-stock was brought up to pasture. The path is steep initially but is easy to follow and is much kinder on your limbs than the track.

Eventually you enter a long meadow which offers good views of the attractive Sierra de Cocón in the distance to the N. Leave the meadow and follow the path N until it climbs up slightly and joins the **PR-PNPE 28** (14.8km; 1400m). Follow this down to the car park and the start of the route.

Following their legal obligation, the park authority has put up a sign indicating that the water quality is not guaranteed. Despite this, I'd have no qualms about drinking here.

WALK 15
Pico de San Carlos

Start/Finish	Joyu el Teju (1300m)
Distance	15.2km
Ascent/Descent	1080m
Grade	Difficult
Time	7–8hr
Terrain	Good tracks to start and finish. Mostly trackless after the Providencia mines.
Map	Editorial Alpina, 1:25,000. Picos de Europa, Macizo Central y Oriental
Access	Follow the CA-1 from Poncebos to Sotres. Drive up through the village and so on up to parking at the Joyu el Teju.
Route finding	Generally easy. Some care needed on leaving the mines.

This is a very satisfying day. The ascent from the Providencia mine ruins to the Silla del Caballo col feels a little wild, but the rewards on reaching the col more than make up for the work put in. The upper reaches of the Liébana valley lie at your feet, over a thousand dizzying metres below, and the ascent of the nearby Pico de San Carlos only serves to heighten the experience. The day can easily be shortened by spending the night at the Ándara refuge.

Follow **PR-PNPE 28** south from the car park (1300m) to reach the **Ándara hut**. (3.6km; 1725m). The track climbs gently, though without respite, to reach the refuge, providing excellent views NE to the Sierra Cocón.

> The **Casetón de Ándara** refuge was originally built by the Mazarrasa company as part of the mining operations that have so strongly affected the Eastern Massif. Remodelled relatively recently, it now serves as a base for walks in what is still the most neglected of the three Picos massifs.

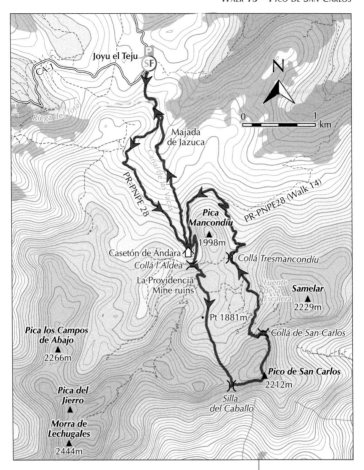

From the hut take the old miners' track that heads
first N and then doubles back S to cross above the hut
itself and reach the **Collá l'Aldea** (4.2km; 1790m) with
its odd, walled pond. Leave the main track here on paths
that climb SE past fenced-off mine workings and on up
into a broad, stony gully. At the head of the gully and

113

the last of the mine workings, take a good path that rises gently R out of the gully then swings round to eventually head S over level ground to reach the ruins of **La Providencia mines** (5.0k; 1890m).

The **Sociedad La Providencia** was the first mine company to operate in the Eastern Massif, and the last to close. From 1859 to 1931 the Providencia extracted zinc ore, initially for the lead it contained and later for the value of the zinc itself. The ore lay in veins sometimes as much as 3m wide, but even so, the work of extracting the ore was truly arduous. Dormitories, a canteen, workshops and even a chapel were built to accommodate the workforce, which included men and women. The men mined the ore and the women collected it at the mouth of each mine, then loaded it onto ox-carts for the long journey down to La Hermida, over 15km away and 1700m lower down the mountain.

At the Providencia mine ruins with the Silla del Caballo col in the far distance

Leave the mine ruins past the remains of a series of old buildings heading S to Spot Height 1881m, which is perfectly situated between two deep *jous* (karst depressions). Once here, take a bearing on the Silla del Caballo, the col due W of the summit of the Pico de San Carlos. Now descend into a stony gully and follow this to the foot of a broad scree that rises to the **Silla del Caballo** (6.4km; 2090m). Struggle up the scree to the col, which provides magnificent views of the Upper Liébana valley.

From the col, turn E and climb the easy-angled, rocky slope to the summit of the **Pico de San Carlos** (7km; 2212m), and an even wider panorama of Potes and the Liébana valley. ▶ When ready, descend N from the summit staying close to the ridge on a good path. At the **Collá de San Carlos** (7.7km; 2052m) drop down W quite steeply at first, and to the L of a heavily mined spur. When the steepness eases follow the track N to the **Fuente de la Escalera** (8.6km; 1890m).

The Pico de San Carlos is also known by locals from the Liébana area as the Sagrado Corazón (Sacred Heart).

> The **Fuente de la Escalera**, in addition to abundant refreshing water, is a botanist's paradise, especially for the species that thrive on the boggy ground just above the spring itself. The stream below the spring also attracts the beautiful Adonis blue butterfly.

Head N from the Escalera spring, and go over the **Collá Tresmancondíu** (9.5km; 1817m) and down the cart track to the junction with **PR-PNPE 28** (11km; 1640m; see Walk 16). Turn L and follow the cart track round the N side of the Mancondíu to the **Ándara refuge** (12.1km; 1725m). Here it is possible to follow the track down to the Joyu el Teju by the way you came up in the morning. However, a far more satisfying to end the day is to drop N off the track into the **Canal de las Vacas** (as for Walk 16). Follow a narrow but quite well-used path and work your way down the bed of the grassy gully, and then out onto the small meadows of the **Majada de Jazuca** (13.9km; 1390m). Here climb out N to re-join the main track not far from the car park and the end of the route.

WALK 16
Pica el Jierru

Start/Finish	Joyu el Teju
Distance	18.1km
Ascent/Descent	1190m
Grade	Very difficult
Time	7–9hr
Terrain	Difficult high-mountain terrain throughout most of the central section.
Map	Editorial Alpina, 1:25,000. Picos de Europa, Macizo Central y Oriental
Access	Follow the CA-1 from Poncebos to Sotres. Drive up through the village and so on up to parking at the Joyu el Teju.
Route finding	Care needed at different points throughout.

Perhaps it's because this was my first full Picos outing after the easing of the 2020 coronavirus lockdown, that for me this is one of the best walks in the guide. It is varied, it is airy and exciting in a couple of places, and it offers outstanding views of the Central Massif from the summit of Pica el Jierro. In addition, it is steeped in history and gives an intimate view of the remains of the mine workings that characterise the Eastern Massif. As with Walk 15, the day can be shortened by spending the night at the Ándara refuge.

From the **Joyu el Teju** car park follow the PR-PNPE 28 to the **Casetón de Ándara** (3.6km; 1725m). Follow the old miners' track above the hut to reach the **Collá l'Aldea** (4.2km; 1790m). Leave the main track here on paths that climb SE past fenced-off mine workings and on up into a broad, stony gully. At the head of the gully, take a good path that rises gently R out of the gully, then swings round to eventually head S over level ground in the direction of La Providencia mines.

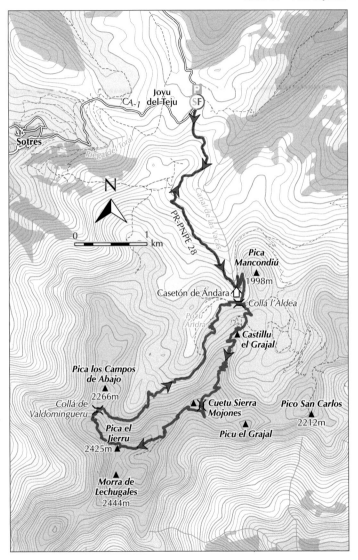

Joyu del Teju

CA-1

Sotres

Riega del Toral

N

0   1 km

PR-PNPE 28

Canal de las Vacas

Pica Mancondiú
1998m

Casetón de Ándara
Collá l'Aldea

Pozu Ándara

Castillu el Grajal

Pica los Campos de Abajo
2266m

Collá de Valdomingueru

Cuetu Sierra Mojones

Pico San Carlos
2212m

Pica el Jierru
2425m

Picu el Grajal

Morra de Lechugales
2444m

All of the above is the same as for Walk 15. However, just before dropping down to the ruined buildings of the Providencia, take the cart track that climbs away R towards the **Castillu el Grajal** (5km; 1883m). The track disappears in some places and the ground is littered with very deep mine shafts which are entertaining but potentially dangerous. Once above the mine shafts, follow the track as it goes around the N spur of the Castillu el Grajal. When the track divides (5.5km; 1935m) take the L fork and follow a cairned path that goes up between the Castillu el Grajal summit on the L and the Cuesta el Grajal ridge on the R. You are now starting the Rasa la Inagotable. ◀

The Rasa la Inagotable refers to the inclined plane the walk now follows and that gave miners a seemingly endless (inagotable) vein of zinc and lead ores.

Ignoring a track that goes off R, follow the main track comfortably as it zig-zags up to the Mesa el Grajal (7.3km; 2210m), a broad grassy col to the NE of the **Picu el Grajal**, an easy optional summit for the day. Descend from the col on the miners' track enjoying excellent views SW of the Upper Liébana valley and beyond that to the Cordillera Cantábrica. Once below the Cuetu Sierra Mojones, abandon the track and climb up onto the ridge on your R, which runs from the summit of the **Cuetu Sierra Mojones** to the Pica el Jierru (7.9km; 2193m).

The cart track that climbs away from the Providencia mines towards the Castillu el Grajal

The ridge is airy and exposed at first and taken mostly on the R side. When it broadens out and the miners' track comes to an end, ignore a steep gully off L and head SW along the main ridge, with a second narrow section taken this time on the L. Cairns and occasional red paint dots help with the navigation over this whole section and lead finally to the **Pica el Jierru** summit (9.3km; 2425m). ▶

The miners' track stops because the 'Inagotable' finally ran out, although it did so at over 2000m, as the mine entrances on the ridge confirm.

The **summit views from the Pica el Jierru** are outstanding, especially those of the Central Massif to the W, with Torrecerredo, the highest summit in the Picos de Europa, clearly visible. The summit block of the Morra de Lechugales, the highest peak in the Eastern Massif, is also clearly visible to the S, with Peña Vieja and the Puertos de Áliva to the SW (Walks 24 and 25). A huge swathe of the Cantabrian coast is visible to the N.

From the summit, go north 50m to a low windbreak from where a cairned path leads away initially NW. The descent is increasingly steep; stay near the edge of the NE spur coming down from the summit as you lose height. Do not be tempted down gullies to the R. At a deep gash (9.7km; 2280m), drop down R then traverse over uncomfortable, broken ground until you can access the grassy slopes of the Campos de Valdomigueru, and from there the **Collá de Valdomingueru** itself (10.3km; 2144m). This is the end of the trickiest part of the route.

From just below the col a cairned path with red paint dots works around the S side of the Joyu Llarosu. Follow the path NE below the Cuesta el Grajal, and then more steeply down and through multiple old shafts and above the dried-out bed of the **Pozu Andra**. Shortly after the mines shafts you come to the **Collá l'Aldea** (14km; 1790m) and rejoin the morning's route. Descend to the Casetón, and then down the **PR-PNPE 28** to **Joyu el Teju** and the car park.

Originally, the whole of the **Pozu Andra valley** was a mountain lake up to 15m deep in places. The lake appears in old sketches of the area in the 19th century, when it was the highest lake in the Picos, and one of the biggest. Unfortunately, blasting in the nearby Mazarrasa mines drained the lake in 1911. After a study in 2012, it was decided that the operations required to restore the lake to its original condition were too risky in environmental terms.

WALK 17
Colláu Cambureru

Start/Finish	Los Invernales del Texu
Distance	14.5km
Ascent/Descent	1300m
Grade	Very difficult
Time	7–9hr
Terrain	Steep in ascent and descent. Rough except for the start and finish tracks.
Map	Editorial Alpina, 1:25,000. Picos de Europa, Macizo Central y Oriental
Access	Follow the CA-1 from Poncebos to Sotres. At a hairpin bend just before Sotres a good track drops off R (S). Follow this for 1km to reach the Invernales del Texu. Park at the track side or above the first cabins of the Invernales del Texu. Alternatively, park in Arenas or Poncebos and use the bus service that runs up to Tielve and Sotres (see Appendix A).
Route finding	Briefly problematic during the ascent to Cambureru.

It might seem odd for the aim of a walk to be a col, but this is a col with a difference. Firstly, it provides good access to Peña Castil, a walkers' summit that offers a bird's-eye view of El Naranjo de Bulnes. In addition, there is the easier option of visiting the Cueva del Hielo, a nearby cave with permanent ice flows. Finally, although this is a long day, the walk allows you to get a real feel for the high-mountain scenery of the Picos, and to get a taste of the rougher Picos terrain.

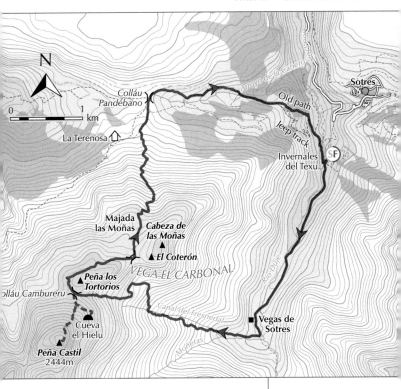

From the **Invernales del Texu** follow the track S for almost 3km to the **Vegas de Sotres**. ▶

There is a good spring just after you ford the River Duje (2.4km; 1040m). Take advantage of this since there is no guarantee of water beyond this point. Immediately after the last of the cabins and livestock pens (3.3km), there is a good view W up the Canal del Fresnedal to the Colláu Cambureru 1000m above. The way ahead looks daunting, but don't allow that to put you off. ▶

Initially the path is faint, but it soon improves and works its way up the L side of the dry **Canal del Fresnedal**. The exact route is vague in places but eventually it

Invernales are winter quarters for livestock, whereas vegas are usually summer pastures.

A fresno is an ash, so a fresnedal is a valley of ash trees. For whatever reason, the trees have long since gone.

121

El Naranjo de Bulnes from the gash by the Peña los Tortorios

becomes easier to cross the gully bed (4.7km; 1580m) to the R side and work up a steep slope to a grassy col (1720m) overlooking the **Vega El Carbonal**. Things get interesting here as you descend N into the hollow of the Carbonal, then swing W over the rocky ground below the S walls of **El Coterón**.

It is easy to see *rebeco* here, and with the Vegas de Sotres and the ascent route completely hidden from you, the sense of remoteness is very strong. The W walls of the Eastern Massif that have accompanied you so far are also hidden from view. You're alone and out of sight.

After passing a small cave off to the R, the route works back over more rocky ground to reach a second grassy col (5.6km; 1810m) and superb views NW down to the morning's work on the ascent from the Vegas de Sotres. The way ahead up to the Colláu Cambureru is now painfully obvious, and until mid-season is often capped with snow. But the worst is almost over, and another 40 minutes or so should see you on the col (6.5km; 2052m), with the first of a number of surprising views of the north face of El Naranjo de Bulnes or Picu Urriellu. ▸

From 1855 to 1872 various teams of **military surveyors** were active in Northern Spain, carrying out mapping work and setting up primitive geodetic positions. In doing so they were responsible for the first ascents of a number of major summits, including the Pica del Jierro (Walk 16) and the Pico Cortés in the Eastern Massif, and Peña Castil in the Central. Whilst not strictly ascents in the sporting sense of the word mountaineering, the work of these teams was still very important as it represented a first approach to the mapping of the area.

Option A – Peña Castil (2444m)

From the col follow a good path up the N slopes of **Peña Castil**. The summit provides outstanding views of the Eastern and Central massifs, and excellent views of

El Naranjo's celebrated summit seems to be just a stones' throw away, as do those of the Neverón de Urreillu and the Pico de Albo group.

The ascent of Peña Castil from the Colláu Cambureru

the coast and beaches of Cantabria to the NE. Above all, though, it offers a bird's-eye view of El Naranjo de Bulnes. On a good day, climbers can be seen quite clearly on the east face. This option adds 2km and 390m of ascent and descent to the day.

Option B – Cueva el Hielu

From the **Colláu Cambureru** head south as for Peña Castil, but after some 40–50m of ascent start to head ESE for some 250m on a poorly defined path with occasional small cairns. Finally swing S to reach the cave entrance. Early in the season you might need crampons to enter the cave. This option adds 1km and 80m of ascent and descent to the day.

Main route

Leave the Colláu Cambureru heading NW on a path that climbs up the rocky W spur of **Peña los Tortorios** (2147m). Follow the path to a narrow gash, just before which there are excellent views back to El Naranjo de Bulnes. The true spectacle, however, comes on crossing the gash (6.9km; 2040m). On a good day you can see over 100km of coastline, from the Sueve mountain range to the NW to the sands of the beach of Oyambre to the NE. Moreover, following the Tortorios spur W for 30m will give you breathtaking views down to Bulnes village, some 1300m below. Very few places allow you to see Bulnes and El Naranjo de Bulnes at the same time.

Now head ENE over grassy slopes and on a narrow, comfortable path, crossing snow patches early in the season. The path comes close to two minor cols (7.9km; 1960m) to the W of the summit of **El Coterón**. It is worth going up to the R-hand col (1973m) as it offers a superb view of the morning's ascent all the way down to the jeep track at the Vegas de Sotres. You are allowed to stop for a while to gloat over your accomplishment.

Back from the col, swing N and descend steeply into the **Majada las Moñas**. Today it's almost impossible to understand the importance of good pastures to the shepherds of the past. But it was sufficient for them to build the sort of paths that will lead you steeply back down to the Colláu Pandébano, provided you locate a good cairn in the N corner of the *majada* (8.6km; 1850m). This cairn marks the start of the descent. Be sure to locate it correctly.

The path down to the **Pandébano** (10.9km; 1215m) is steep and rocky in a number of places and should not be rushed. Towards the end, however, things level out nicely and, if you have time, don't think twice about stopping at **La Terenosa refuge** for refreshment. You deserve it.

From Pandébano descend E to the jeep track that comes up from Sotres and follow this down E. Just when the track is about to start its merciless zig-zag down to the Invernales del Texu, on your L there is, illogically, a double gate to an unfenced field (12.9km; 1030m). Dropping away between the gate and the main track is the start of the old, cobbled drove road that used to link Pandébano to the Invernales. This is worth locating as it is shorter and far more pleasant than the jeep track itself, which is joined just in time to reach the **Invernales del Texu** and the end of the walk.

(The walk to and from the Colláu Cambureru was recommended to me by professional guide Juanjo Álvarez of Casa Cipriano in Sotres.)

WALK 18
Cabrones and Urriellu

Start/Finish	Bulnes
Distance	16.1km
Ascent/Descent	1800m
Grade	Very difficult
Time	2 days
Terrain	Frequently steep, rough and trackless. There are short, exposed scrambles in two places.
Map	Editorial Alpina, 1:25,000. Picos de Europa, Macizo Central y Oriental
Access	From Las Arenas de Cabrales, follow the AS-264 to Poncebos. There is parking at the lower funicular station if you are very lucky, or on the roadside around or before Poncebos. Alternatively take the summer bus service from Arenas to Poncebos (see Appendix A).
Route finding	Not difficult except for the top section of Day 1. The route to Cabrones is PR-PNPE 18, and from the hut in Urriellu it is PR-PNPE 19.

The Pico de Albo summit dominates the view of the Central Massif from anywhere north of the Picos, and yet is very seldom climbed. Instead, it acts as an axis around which this excellent two-day walk rotates. The first day ends at the wild, remote but magnificent Jou de los Cabrones, home to the highest mountain hut in Spain. The second goes past Spain's most famous hut at the foot of the great west face of El Naranjo de Bulnes. Tough walking with a steep ascent and an even steeper descent, but great views and, for good or for bad, an unforgettable experience.

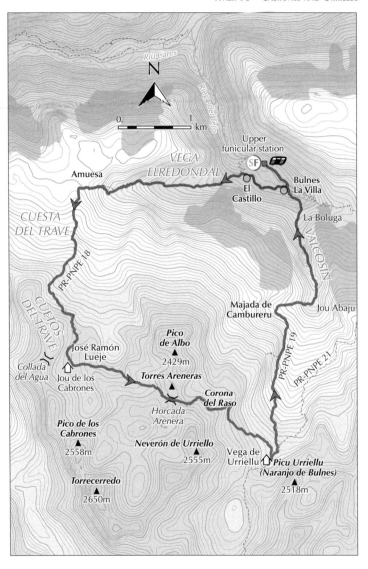

DAY 1
Bulnes to Jou de los Cabrones

Start	Bulnes
Finish	Jou de los Cabrones (José Ramón Lueje hut)
Distance	7.5km
Ascent/Descent	1485m/70m

Take the funicular from Poncebos to Bulnes or walk up on the old path (and add two hours to Day 1). From the exit of the **funicular railway station**, walk up to **Bulnes La Villa**, the lower village (0.4km; 650m). After refreshments and a tour of the scatter of houses, follow **PR-PNPE 18** up and through **El Castillo**, the upper village. An information board points you towards Amuesa and Cabrones. Go past the Fuente del Tornu (2km; 855m), and then cross the **Vega el Redondal**, and the last of the level ground.

Amuesa yields excellent views across the Cares Gorge to the Western Massif, as well as back down to Bulnes and across to Pandébano.

The path up to Amuesa is relentless and it would not be a good idea to be caught here on a hot summer's morning, but the agony ends, eventually, at **Amuesa** (4.2km; 1410m), an open mountain pasture with abandoned cabins. ◄

From Amuesa, turn S and follow a narrow path up the broad, grassy **Cuesta del Trave** spur. Initially the path stays mostly to the R of the spur before it comes out onto the crest itself (5.4km; 1770m). Follow this briefly on a grassy slope, but abandon it just before the highest point of the grass (5.6km; 1820m) and take to the less inviting rocky ground to the L.

Route finding can be tricky over the next section, especially, when crossing blank, slabby sections. Look out for small cairns and for the muddy scuff marks left by boots. Be prepared to cross patches of old snow until mid-summer.

The intermittent path first climbs generally S and then swings SE and traverses high up below the Trave walls. Eventually you are forced to scramble up to a tiny

col (ropes) (6.7km; 2025m). The reward for your trials is a sudden but superb view of the Pico and Agujas de Cabrones to the S.

Turn S at the col and follow the path over uncomfortable, rocky ground with more ropes to safeguard the passage below the walls of the **Cueto del Trave Oriental**. When the **José Ramón Lueje hut** comes into view the worst is over, and it only remains to amble down round the NW rim of the **Jou de los Cabrones**.

On a good evening, walkers staying in the Lueje hut will make their way up to the Collada del Agua (2140m). The view of the Western Massif is spectacular. Equally impressive is the **Canal del Agua**, which falls almost 1800m from the col to the River Cares below.

José Ramón Lueje was a connoisseur of the mountains of Asturias and León, particularly the Picos de Europa. A tax inspector by profession, during the

Crossing slabby ground below the Cuetos del Trave

Arriving at the José Ramón Lueje hut in the Jou de los Cabrones

middle part of the 20th century he photographed both the landscapes of these mountains and the people that inhabited them. This passion left us today with an invaluable collection of over 14,000 black and white photographs of shepherds, farmers and local people either in their villages or the *majadas* and *brañas* of the summer pastures.

The hut in the Jou de los Cabrones was named in honour of Lueje. It is the most remote hut in Spain and has twice been completely destroyed by avalanches. The sleeping quarters of the current structure are from a structure that was built in 1981 and then later enlarged.

DAY 2
Jou de los Cabrones to Bulnes

Start	Jou de los Cabrones (José Ramón Lueje hut)
Finish	Bulnes
Distance	8.6km
Ascent/Descent	315m/1730m

From the hut go E and gain the col at Spot Height 2022. The Horcada Arenera is now clearly visible between the

Neverón de Urriello and the **Torres Areneras** and the way ahead is obvious. Follow the vague path guided by small cairns and blue and green paint spots. There will be snow over this section well into June some years and the feeling of remoteness is almost oppressive. The arrival at the **Horcada Arenera** (1.9km; 2273m) comes as a relief, even though there is quite a bit of work still to do today. ▶

From the col, contour round below the N spur of the Neverón de Urriello on a better path. This leads to the **Corona del Raso** (2.8km; 2180m), a shoulder on the NE spur of the Neverón that offers stunning views of the towering west face of El Naranjo de Bulnes, or Picu Urriellu as it is known today. Despite the recent addition of metal rungs, the descent of the chimney-groove at the Corona del Raso needs care as a fall would have very serious consequences. Once down, however, a narrow path leads off SW and then S and the terrain becomes more amenable, although never exactly comfortable except for the last couple of hundred metres just before arriving at the **Vega de Urriellu hut** (4km; 1960m).

On a clear day, the Arenera col offers good views ENE over the northern reaches of the Picos to the beaches on the coast of Cantabria.

SPANISH ALPINISM

Alpinism in Spain came of age on 5 August 1904 when Pedro Pidal, the Marquis of Villaviciosa, reached the summit of El Naranjo de Bulnes for the first time. He was assisted in his venture by Gregorio Pérez, 'El Cainejo', a shepherd from the village of Caín. Their ascent was a remarkable affair.

On 2 August word was sent to El Cainejo asking him to join the Marquis in Ario in the Western Massif. He did so by leaving Caín after supper and making the approach by moonlight. Arriving at dawn the following day, he and the Marquis set off for the Torre de Santa María (2476m), which they climbed prior to summiting on Peña Santa de Castilla (2596m). That evening they slept in Ario and the next day descended the Canal de Trea, crossed the Cares Gorge and climbed up the Canal de Piedravellida. From the Collado de Cerredo they traversed above Bulnes and dropped down into the Majada de Camburero, where they spent the night. The following morning, they made their historic ascent, drank a bottle of wine on the summit, left a note in the empty bottle, and left a second bottle for the second ascensionist. The next day they returned home having made the most important first ascent in the history of Spanish alpinism.

From the hut ignore PR-PNPE 21, the main path going off down to Pandébano, and head due N across the meadow, past a large bivouac boulder to pick up an intermittent path, the **PR-PNPE 19**. This works its way down among slabby rocks until it comes out onto the screes below the E walls of El Frailón (1km; 1710m). Descend the screes on a well-used path and follow this to where it swings W and enters the **Majada de Cambureru** (2.2km; 1335m).

Looking back at the Picu Urriellu in the afternoon sun, it is not difficult to see where the name **Naranjo de Bulnes** might have come from. *Naranjo* means 'orange'. Much harder to grasp is that, until 1935, there were enough shepherds at Cambureru to sustain a bar, a *pensión*, and a skittles alley! Sadly, today everything lies in ruins.

From Cambureru descend steeply E down the Canal de Cambureru, which comes out in a grassy glacial cirque, the **Jou Abaju** (3km; 1080m). Here the path swings N and enters the **Valcosín**, a broad grassy vale that ends in **La Boluga**, a gorge where you are forced to walk along the bed of the river. On coming out of the gorge, go R 30m or so and descend a small rocky mound before coming back L and crossing the river below a waterfall. This last section can be problematic after heavy rain. **Bulnes** lies below a few minutes away (4.7km; 650m). If you want to, queue for the next funicular, but if you have the energy, walk down the old path. It only takes an hour and is the true finish to this inspiring walk.

LIÉBANA

Mogrovejo and the 8th-century tower with the Eastern Massif in the background (Walk 26)

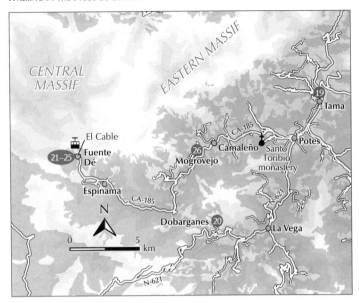

Much as I love the Asturian side of the Picos having lived there these last 40 plus years, there is no denying the Liébana valley is especially attractive for visitors to the Picos. One of the attractions is the almost Mediterranean climate, due to the valley lying in a marked rain shadow. Liébana is the only place in the Picos where grapes are cultivated for wine-making, for example, and it enjoys more dry, sunny days than any other part of the range. The other major attraction of the Liébana is the wealth of gentler walks in and around the tiny villages that dot the northern slopes of the valley in particular. Finally, the cable car at Fuente Dé can whisk you

up to 1800m in a matter of minutes and give you easy access to the high-mountain terrain of the Central Massif of the Picos.

Potes, the capital of the Liébana valley, is a busy, sometimes crowded, but undeniably important tourist centre. As with Cangas de Onís and Arenas de Cabrales, it offers all the services visitors might need, including banks, supermarkets, shops, equipment stores, a post office, bars, restaurants and tourist information facilities. There is an extensive range of accommodation both in Potes and in the many villages strung out along the length of the valley. There are campsites at La Viorna (above

Potes), Turieno (2km from Potes on the Espinama road); in San Pelayo (5km from Potes on the Espinama road) and, my own favourite, in the woods behind the cable car at Fuente Dé.

The two major tourist attractions in the Liébana valley are, in stark contrast the one with the other, the Santo Toribio monastery and its piece of the true cross, and the cable car at Fuente Dé, with its heart-stopping, totally unsupported journey up more than 700m metres to El Cable, the upper station. Depending on which attraction you choose, the experience will be spiritually or otherwise uplifting. However, for anyone looking for a more earthly experience, then a visit to the "Sotama" National Park visitor centre in Tama, just N of Potes, would be an excellent idea. The centre has various permanent displays explaining different aspects of the Picos de Europa and is especially good for the coverage it gives of mining over the centuries.

For anyone travelling without their own transport, buses from Santander currently run twice a day run through Unquera and Panes, and then on to Potes via the spectacular Hermida Gorge. During the summer months the route from Santander is extended up the valley, through Espinama to Fuente Dé. For details see www.autobusespalomera.com. There are numerous taxi firms in the Potes area. Tickets for the cable car can be booked online at https://entra das.telefericofuentede.com. Booking in advance is a wise precaution in July and August.

The Canal de Pedavejo goes up between the Torre Salinas (top L) and the Torre de la Regaliz (top R) (Walk 21)

WALK 19

Pueblos de Liébana

Start/Finish	Sewage treatment plant, Tama (240m).
Distance	13.5km
Ascent/Descent	630m
Grade	Moderate
Time	5–6hr
Terrain	Mainly tracks and well-used paths. One short section on tarmac.
Map	Adrados Ediciones, 1:50,000. Parque Nacional de los Picos de Europa
Access	From the S end of Tama, go W over the River Deva, turn R and follow the road N for some 700m. The main road swings up W here, but go R and continue N for 1km to good parking next to the sewage treatment plant for Liébana.
Route finding	Mostly straightforward. Some care needed in the villages and at a couple of intersections of tracks.

The cable car at Fuente Dé exerts an enormous pull over visitors to Liébana, who mostly rush past the lower section of the valley spellbound by the high summits. But the Picos de Europa are mountains from the highest summits to the lowest foothills. This walk ventures into these foothills and combines a visit to various villages and hamlets with walking through rich and varied woodlands. On walks like this, poorer weather does not mean a poor walk.

Very soon after leaving the **sewage treatment plant** (*depuradora*) the tarmac ends and you come to a clearing by a river. Cross the river on a simple, wooden bridge and, immediately after, take the L fork at a small chapel and start to climb NW on an old track. This is waymarked with a shell, the sign of the Camino de Santiago, and a red cross, the sign for the Camino Lebaniego.

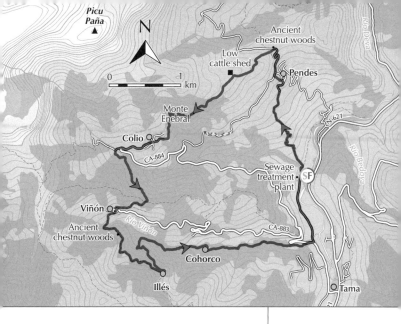

The track climbs quite steeply in places, but offers excellent views of the Eastern Massif of the Picos de Europa to the W and, in the opposite direction, to the

Walking up through Colio with Peña Ventoso beyond

rock walls and ridges that descend dramatically from Peña Ventosa to the Hermida Gorge.

After a steep middle section the trail eases off and enters **Pendes** (1.6km; 440m). Walk up through the village until, above the last of the houses, you come out onto a road. Turn R (N) and follow the road up two hairpins to a livestock pen on the L (2.5km; 540m). Take the jeep track that goes gently up in an WSW direction. It climbs to a long, **low cattle shed** on your R. Leave the track here and cross SW over open land on a much vaguer track. This quickly descends towards woodland, crosses a cattle grid, and enters the woods.

> The **woods** are a mixture of holm oak, with its tiny, holly-like leaves, and Pyrenean oak, with its large, heavily lobulated leaves. Both species are indicators of the warm dry climate typical of Mediterranean Spain, and, surprisingly, of the Liébana valley.

Follow the trail as it descends through the ancient woodland of the **Monte Enebral** before coming out suddenly at a tiny chapel of San Roque on the E limit of Colio (4.9km; 560m). Walk WSW through the village, taking time to admire the architecture, old and new, and on down the **CA-884** road to the bus stop (5.7km; 550m). Go R here, cross the river, and immediately after that leave the road and descend L (S) on an old track. This leads essentially SE through mature woodland. When it climbs up to a four-way junction (6.7km; 630m), go straight across and descend SW to come out in **Viñón** (7.2km; 570m) at a junction next to the village washing sheds.

Turn L on reaching the road in Viñón, go past the washing sheds, and then turn immediately R and walk down among traditional houses, some restored and others sadly in ruins. Leave the village heading W on a good track. This contours round through mature woodland, with a number of ups and downs, but heading essentially SE.

Look out for the ancient **chestnuts**. Some are hundreds of years old and many are enormous at the base, but almost all have been heavily coppiced over time to generate fresh growth. Chestnuts were food for the local people in past times, and also for farm animals, especially pigs.

The woodland track comes out at a hairpin in a concrete track (9km; 570m) on the N edge of **Illés**. Go down 10m or so and then swing back L and follow a wide grassy path W and gently down back into the woods. At one point (9.7km; 500m) the path doubles back on itself and goes N briefly, but then descends mainly E above the true right bank of the **Río Viñón** until it reaches **Cohorco**. ▶

The sensation of being in a time warp increases as this walk progresses, but reaches its maximum expression in the tiny hamlet of Cohorco.

Descending the grassy path just after Illés

Pass through Cohorco (10.8km; 350m), cross a stream, and follow a track to a junction. Take the L fork and descend above the River Viñón on a good path. Just after a large cattle shed on the L (12.3km; 280m), come out onto the **CA-883** road. Follow this E for 80m or so and then turn L and walk N to get to the start of the route.

CAMINO LEBANIEGO AND THE CAMINO VANDINIENSE

As you make your way up to Pendes, you will probably encounter walkers heading in the opposite direction. They are following either the Camino Lebaniego or the Camino Vandiniense. The first of these was taken by Medieval pilgrims who wished to visit the monastery at Santo Toribio de Liébana, just above Potes. The monastery is home to the largest known piece of the Lignum Crucis, the True Cross, and is well worth a visit. In addition, if you can arrange transport, an excellent route for a day of doubtful weather is to join the Camino Lebaniego at the tiny village of Lebeña, some 4km north of Tama. Here, the wonderful, 10th-century church of Santa María de Lebeña is worth a visit in its own right, regardless of the weather, and lies on the final section of the Lebaniego Way.

The Camino Vandiniense is one of the many variations on the Camino de Santiago (The Way of Saint James). Starting in San Vicente de la Barquera on the coast of Cantabria, this pilgrims' trail links the Camino del Norte, which reaches Santiago de Compostela along the Cantabrian coast, with the Camino Francés, which crosses the plains of the north of Castilla y León and is the most popular route to Santiago today.

Viñón

WALK 20

Pico Jano

Start/Finish	Dobarganes
Distance	9.2km
Ascent/Descent	600m
Grade	Moderate
Time	4–5hr
Terrain	Tracks and paths almost throughout. Waymarked.
Map	Adrados Ediciones, 1:50,000. Parque Nacional de los Picos de Europa
Access	Follow the N621 road from Potes in the direction of the Puerto de San Glorio until, after 14km, Dobarganes is signposted off to the R. Drive up to the village.
Parking	Park on the L just after the first houses, near the rubbish collection point.

This walk takes you out of the Picos to allow you to look in at them and try to disentangle their complexity. The walk gives you superb views of both the Eastern Massif and the Fuente Dé area of the Central Massif. But the walk up and then down through extensive oak woods would justify the outing even without the views. Also fascinating is the human story behind the Dobarganes we see today. All in all, it's a great shorter day.

There is an information board to the L of the village refuse collection containers. The route map on the board is accurate and worth a moment of your time. Then go up the lane to the L of the board and climb up into the superb oak forests that carpet the slopes of the whole valley. Join a track (0.3km; 1020m) and follow this up through mature woodland. ▸

The track leads W to the **La Tejera reservoir** (1.3km; 1100m). Skirt around the L side of the reservoir and then follow a path as it climbs essentially NNW, crossing a track at one point. Eventually you come out onto the

There is an Iron Age hill fort, the Castro de Llan de la Peña, just off to the R some 600m into the walk.

141

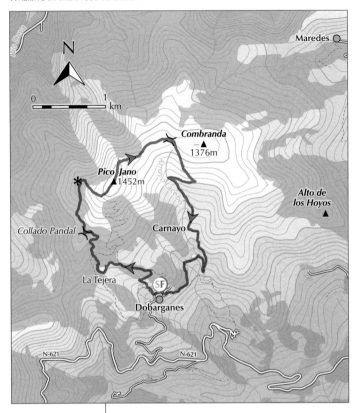

wooded **Collado Pandal** (2.4km; 1230m). Notice here
how in the space of less than 50m the trees change dramatically from oak to beech as the walk takes you over
from the Dobarganes side and down along the colder
north-facing slopes above the Liébana valley.

Oak and beech woods abound in the Picos de
Europa, but prefer quite different soils and climates.
Beech needs cool, humid north-facing slopes,
while the oaks, particularly the Pyrenean oak found

on the mountain sides of N Spain, prefers drier, more southerly slopes. The influence of soil and slope can be seen in many places through the Picos de Europa.

The path contours idyllically N through the beech woods and offers tantalising glimpses of the main Picos summits. The idyll doesn't last long, however, and suddenly you are obliged to climb steadily through the upper reaches of the beech woods until, at a small clearing, you get your first views of the Fuente Dé area, with Peña Remoña, the Tornos de Liordes and the Alto la Padierna (Walks 21 and 22) easily picked out to the W.

Contour briefly round then climb steadily SE, this time through giant broom and heather. When you reach a track coming up from the R (3.7km; 1390m), turn L and follow it to the summit of **Pico Jano** (4km; 1452m). The views are superb in all directions, but especially north to the Eastern Massif.

Leave the summit heading first NNE and then later swinging E to reach a broad col (5.2km; 1325m).

The Pico Jano summit with the Eastern Massif shrouded in cloud beyond

The **Combranda** summit a little further on is home to a Megalithic necropolis. Descend R at this point and work down through tall broom, and then on into the oak woods, now on a track. Following waymarking, abandon the track to the R (5.8km; 1210m) and contour round on a livestock path to the **Arroyo Lacebo** gully. Descend steeply keeping the gully on the R until you come to an old barn at **Carnayo**.

Just after the barn (7.1km; 1030m) follow a track steeply down until the waymarking indicates a sharp right turn (7.9km; 920m) and another tarn is reached. More than for the need to rest, it is tempting to prolong the outing and stay here for a while. However, when you are ready to face the rigours of the outside world, follow the wooded track pleasantly back to **Dobarganes**.

TEJERA RESERVOIR

In 1982 the Dobarganes Six, as they were known in many places, built the Tejera reservoir with the aim of trebling their meat and dairy production in order to fight their way out of poverty without having to leave their village. The reservoir meant they had water all year round for their livestock, as well as for irrigating fields that provided hay for the winter months. Taking three years to build, the reservoir also triggered off, among other things, the installation of drinking troughs, the telephone, the paving of the village streets, and the road connection to the N-621 road to the San Glorio pass. How often de we sit and moan when the answer to our problems is in our own hands?

WALK 21
Vega de Liordes

Start/Finish	Fuente Dé
Distance	13.2km
Ascent/Descent	1080m
Grade	Difficult
Time	6–7hr
Terrain	Initially a good track, then steep up the Canal de Pedabejo
Map	Edición Alpina, 1:25,000. Picos de Europa, Macizos Central y Oriental
Access	Follow the CA-185 to Fuente Dé from anywhere in the Liébana valley.
Parking	There is car parking all around the cable car complex. Arrive early for easy parking and access to the cable car. Tickets can be bought in advance at https://entradas.telefericofuentede.com.

Vega de Liordes is a superb example of a *polje*, a classic karst feature. This circular walk rotates around Peña Remoña, the eye-catching peak that towers formidably above the meadows at Fuente Dé. This classic walk (PR-PNPE 25) provides a longer day that mixes very different terrains in a memorable journey into the high-mountain landscape of the Picos. The 1000m descent down the Tornos de Liordes using the old miners' track is not something that is easily forgotten, for good or for bad.

From the car park at **Fuente Dé** (1080m) walk S around the W side of the cable car complex. At the end of the tarmacked road, go over a cattle grid and follow a well-used jeep track S, going past the entry point for the delightful **Camping El Redondo**.

Take time to enjoy the beauty of the immense beech woods as the morning light filters through the leaves. Extensive, healthy beech woods carpet the whole of the upper reaches of the Liébana valley creating a

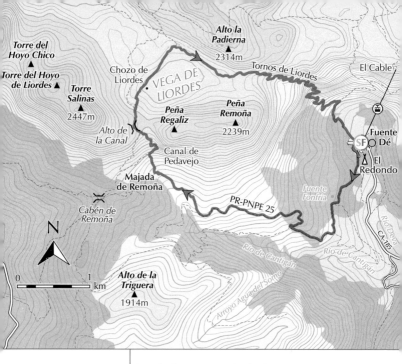

breathtaking sweep of unbroken green from late April through to September.

The track goes momentarily off the Alpina map here, but is waymarked and obvious. First you go past the **Fuente Fonfría** spring, (1.1km; 1175m), and 1km further on past a second spring. A kilometre or so further on again, ignore a track that goes off L (2.2km; 1330m) and climb first NE and then N before swinging W and leaving the beech woods behind for oak scrub. Peña Remoña and the Torre de Alcacero reign over you to the N. ◄

Two kilometres further on (4.3km: 1515m) abandon the track and follow signposting R in order to rise gently across meadows, go through a gate, and continue on towards the **Majada de Remoña** and its solitary hut. A short distance N of the hut (5.3km; 1680m), work N up a tongue of low heather to gain the narrow path that descends from the **Cabén de Remoña** above to the W

This first section is common with the PR-PNPE 15, the Senda del Mercadillo, which comes across from Valdeón (Walk 28).

(Walk 28). Turn right (E) and follow the path as it ascends the vast stone chute that constitutes the lower half of the the **Canal de Pedavejo**.

Work laboriously up the path (abundant waymarking, but some snow early in the season) until the it swings briefly L, crosses a small hollow, and comes out quite suddenly onto a promontory above the Vega de Liordes. The **Alto de la Canal** (6.4km; 2035m) is the highest point on the walk, and an excellent lunch spot.

> This is the view that the Spanish engineer, **Casiano del Prado** would have had in 1853 when he arrived in the Picos to climb the Torre Salinas (Walk 28). He was sure that it was the highest point in the Picos, but from the summit he saw that higher mountains lay to the N. He resolved to return and climb them, but never did.

From the Alto de la Canal descend steeply N (old snow until early summer) to enter the **Vega de Liordes**, and reach the **Chozo de Liordes**, an old shepherd's hut (7.1km; 1880m). Continue N on a good path until it is possible to swing E and then SE below the walls of the **Alto la Padierna** (Walk 22).

> The **Vega de Liordes** is a *polje*. This is a characteristic feature of the middle-mountain landscape in the Picos de Europa. Water from rainfall and snowmelt gathers in a natural hollow or an old glacial cirque, and filters out through sink holes and cave systems that lie below the hollow. In an early stage of the process, the hollow will often fill with enough water to create a shallow lake. Later the lake will begin to cover with vegetation, and in the final stage, the vegetation will cover the lake completely, leaving level, boggy ground that is home to some unique flora. Vega de Liordes has reached this final stage. Walk 3 shows you all three stages in the life of a *polje*.

About to set off down the Tornos de Liordes with Fuente Dé 1000m below

The eastern limit of Vega de Liordes (9km; 1960m) is covered in the remains of mine workings, but what will probably hold your attention most when you reach this side of Liordes is the breathtaking, possibly intimidating, view down to Fuente Dé.

The track you are on was used to ferry provisions up to the Liordes mines, and then carry ore back down to Fuente Dé. If the view down to Fuente Dé makes you feel sorry for yourself, then stop for a moment to think of the miners who had to make this journey on a regular basis. Only then are you allowed to pity yourself as you embark upon what for some is an unnerving, seemingly interminable descent.

Care is needed most of the way down **Los Tornos de Liordes**; time has taken its toll on the old path and some short sections are very loose or have collapsed. When another path comes in from the left (12.3km; 1210m) the worst is over, and it is then an easy matter of ambling down through the woods to the car park at **Fuente Dé**. A drink in the Parador is a good way to end the day, either to celebrate your achievement or to calm shattered nerves.

WALK 22
Alto la Padierna

Start/Finish	Fuente Dé
Distance	16.7km
Ascent/Descent	1410m
Grade	Very difficult
Time	7–9hr
Terrain	Steep in ascent and descent. Exposed and trackless in places.
Map	Editorial Alpina, 1:25,000. Picos de Europa, Macizo Central y Oriental
Access	Follow the CA-185 to Fuente Dé from anywhere in the Liébana valley.
Parking	There is car parking all around the cable car complex. Arrive early for easy parking and access to the cable car. Tickets can be bought in advance at https://entradas.telefericofuentede.com.
Route finding	Easy except for one short section above Liordes.

The steep and tormented Tornos de Liordes miners' track from Fuente Dé is dominated on the L by the summits of Peña Remoña but is defined on the R by the sheer walls of the Alto la Padierna. This diminutive summit is clearly a stunning viewpoint for the whole area. A long walk, with very significant ascent and descent, but with an easy 'opt-out clause' should you run out of steam after getting down from the Padierna.

Start in the main car park for the cable car (1080m) and start early so as to get a good way up the **Tornos de Liordes** before the sun hits them. Reach the Tornos by crossing the meadow N of the car park in a NW direction. The route is waymarked as PR-PNPE 25, but is grimly obvious even from the car park itself. ▸

Countless hairpins on an increasingly rough, exposed track lead to a point under the Alto la Padierna

The constantly changing morning light and expanding horizons will help you forget the pain of the ascent.

summit where the track starts to level out and passes by the remains of the **Mina de Liordes**. Just after the remains, the track levels out completely and rewards you with a superb view of the **Vega de Liordes** (4.2km; 1960m).

> **Mining** in Liordes began in 1872. As with mines elsewhere in the Picos, the miners were after lead. The 32 precision-built hairpins of the Tornos de Liordes were built as a track to evacuate the lead. Unfortunately, the effort was in vain as the lead ore was of poor quality.

Now follow a good path around the NE reaches of the Liordes depression and climb comfortably to **La Padierna** (5.6km; 2020m), the high ground to the NNW of the Vega de Liordes, and the confluence of various walks in the area. The approaches to Collado Jermoso from Cordiñanes (Walk 29) and from the Cabén de Remoña arrive at La Padierna from the W and S, respectively.

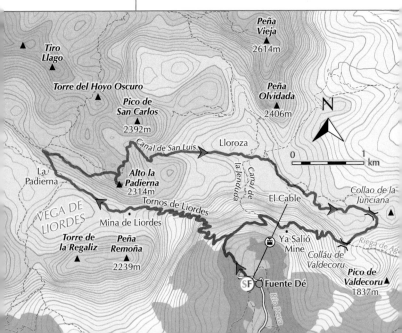

The Alto la Padierna from Fuente Dé

From La Padierna climb steeply NW across rock walls on an exposed path. Near the top of the path a wooden sign points E to the Colladina de las Nieves. ▸ Climb steeply away E from the Collado Jermoso path. The Alto la Padierna summit comes into view almost immediately, but don't head straight for it. Instead follow the slabby ground close to the walls above Liordes. This is the Sedo de la Padierna and is clearly marked on the Editorial Alpina map. The path is vague but the route is marked by frequent small cairns and double red paint flashes. ▸

The path becomes evident again during the final climb up to the Colladina de las Nieves (7.1km; 2251m), and another 10 minutes is all that is needed to gain the **Alto la Padierna** summit and the highpoint of the day (2314m).

Peña Santa de Castilla and the Torre Bermeja dominate the skyline to the W.

It is easy to see herds of rebeco grazing in this area.

151

*Turning to make
the ascent to the
Colladina de las
Nieves, with the Vega
de Liordes below*

The views from the **Alto de la Padierna** are excellent. A huge section of the Cordillera Cantábrica can be seen in the distance to the south. Peña Sagra dominates the skyline in the far distance to the E, whilst Peña Vieja (Walk 24) rises majestically to the NE. The upper cable car station lies at your feet, perched on the edge of a precipice. To the S and W a chain of summits runs from Peña Remoña (Walk 21) over the Torre Salinas (Walk 28) to the Torre Friero, while to the N the Pico de San Carlos helps you to determine the continuation of this walk.

Return to the Colladina de las Nieves and leave it heading NE, using the summit of the Pico de San Carlos as a reference. Red paint marks (dots and stripes) indicate the route, which descends over increasingly slabby rock to the head of the **Canal de San Luis** (8.2km; 2150m). Care is needed over the final section of this descent both with the terrain and navigation. Now descend SE over very rocky terrain until you reach a good path that takes you E. The path skirts round the S side of the **Lloroza** depression and brings you to a point just above the entrance to the **Canal de la Jenduda** (10.2km; 1850m).

Continue E along the path until it joins the miners' track to **El Cable**, the upper cable car station. If you have had enough for the day, you can walk S to the station, join the queue, and then allow the machine to whisk you down to bars and beverages in just under four minutes. Alternatively, to make an already good day great, swing E off the track to the cable car just before El Cable (11km; 1875m) and climb up to a telecommunications mast. From the mast, head ESE over rolling grassy hills until you reach the fence at the **Collao de la Junciana** (12.6km; 1864m). Cross the fence and swing SW to descend rocky ground on a well-used path that ends 10min later at the **Colláu de Valdecoru** (13.3km; 1784m.). ▶

The views down to Fuente Dé and across to Peña Remoña make the extra effort suddenly all worthwhile.

Descend on vague narrow paths, either close to the walls on the R until it is necessary to swing back sharp L (SE), or down a grassy spur on a poor path to just above a rocky outcrop, then N to a better path. Whichever way you descend, take care on the slippery long, broad-bladed grass.

The path now drops steeply down hugging the towering walls of El Cable as it descends to the remains of the **Ya Salió mine**, with its entrances, the original cableway, and the remains of an old hut (14.8km; 1450m). From the hut descend to the junction with the PR-PNPE 25 at the point where you began the gruelling ascent up the Tornos de Liordes in the morning. ▶

Throughout the descent, you are allowed to look up and feel superior to those being mechanically dragged up and down in the cable car.

WALK 23
El Cable and La Jenduda

Start/Finish	Fuente Dé
Distance	9.7km
Ascent/Descent	920m
Grade	Very difficult
Time	5–6hr
Terrain	The descent down La Jenduda is trackless, on steep, unstable rock and scree. Do NOT attempt it unless confident in this type of terrain.
Map	Editorial Alpina, 1:25,000. Picos de Europa, Macizo Central y Oriental
Access	Follow the CA-185 to Fuente Dé from anywhere in the Liébana valley.
Parking	There is car parking all around the cable car complex. Arrive early for easy parking and access to the cable car. Tickets can be bought in advance at https://entradas.telefericofuentede.com.

This spectacular walk follows the old miners' path up to and across the huge walls below the cable car at Fuente Dé. The improbable, airy positions mean that a good head for heights is a must, although the narrow path is well used, and the views of the Fuente Dé cirque are unique. An excellent option when the high peaks are shrouded in cloud, the route has different descents, the easiest being by cable car, and the hardest by La Jenduda, the enormous gash that slices through the walls west of the upper cable car station.

From the car park at **Fuente Dé** (1080m) walk NW across the meadow and pick up **PR-PNPE 25** to Liordes. Abandon this when it strikes off L and follow a broad path towards the huge walls directly below the cable car. At 1.6km (1385m) ignore faint paths that go off L (the descent comes down these) and stay on the main path. This rises E in continually improving positions to a grassy

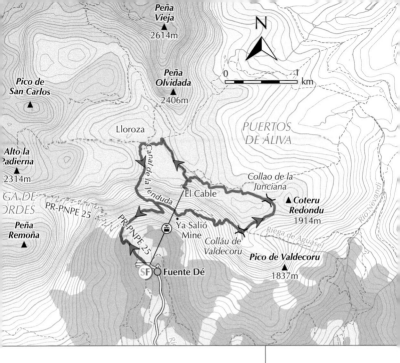

shoulder directly below the *teleférico* cables. The path levels off on reaching the shoulder (2km; 1450m) and goes past a ruined miners' hut, then swings NE and goes past abandoned **Ya Salió mine** entrances.

The first work in the remarkable **Ya Salió mine** was carried out during the first half of the 20th century. The main entrance was made accessible by the path the miners made, and which this route follows up to this point. The zinc ore (sphalerite) was carried down to the washing sheds on a primitive cable car. The remains of this are still visible both below the path near the mine entrance, and down in the Fuente Dé meadows near the Parador. The mine was closed in 1957, and part of the machinery was taken to the Manforas mine in the Puertos de Áliva (Walk 24).

After the mine workings, the path traverses down and round below the huge orange and grey overhangs clearly visible from the car park. Climb away from these on a narrow, exposed path so as to gain an airy, grassy shoulder (2.3km; 1495m). The views vertically down to Fuente Dé are simply wonderful, but are not for those with vertigo. When a narrow but quite well-used path swings L (NW) and sets off back towards the cable car, ignore this. Instead, strike off R on a less evident path and work essentially E up a shaly spur to gain the **Colláu de Valdecoru** (3.3km; 1785m).

The views of Fuente Dé disappear now, and fresh views open up to the NE over the upper reaches of the Liébana valley, and further on to the long spine of Peña Sagra above the Cantabrian coast.

From the Colláu de Valdecoru contour round NE (red dots for waymarking) to reach the **Colláu de la Junciana** (4km; 1864m), a fence, and views over the Puertos de Áliva to the great SE walls of Peña Olvidada and Peña Vieja (Walk 24). Seek out a telecommunications hut that is clearly visible to the W above the upper cable car station. Work across to this on intermittent paths and then make the short descent to the station at **El Cable** (5.7km; 1850m). If the idea of the descent of La Jenduda does not appeal to you, take the cable car down.

The **cable car** at Fuente Dé was opened with great pomp and ceremony in 1966 by General Franco, the Spanish dictator. The idea for a cable car had been put forward in 1961 as a way to promote the Camaleño area for tourism. The work was done by an Italian company, and initially the cabins could carry seven passengers and the operator. Subsequent improvements mean that today each cabin can carry 20 passengers. The 1450m cable overcomes an unsupported 753m height difference in less than four minutes, making it is the third-longest cable car lift in the world.

At the chockstone in the Canal de la Jenduda; metal rungs were placed here in 2022

From the cable car follow the main jeep track N and NW as far as a long bend to the E (6.6km; 1890m). Drop L off the track here, and work W over rocky slabs to a point just S of **Lloroza**. Turn S and gain the entry to **La Jenduda** (7.1km; 1850m). Descend into the upper reaches of the gash and cross a small meadow. This ends abruptly at the head of the gully proper (7.4km; 1790m). The view is not for the faint-hearted – 200m of descent down trackless, unstable screes, rocks and boulders. But this is the worst moment, and very soon you are immersed in the engaging task of choosing the best route down, which is generally on the L. Just as the oppressive gully walls begin to open out, go over completely to the L wall and use ropes and rungs to help you descend the L side of a huge chockstone.

After the descent of the chockstone follow the path across to the R-hand walls and come out of the gully onto open ground. Descend steeply on a narrow, well-used path that is half hidden in the grass. Head in a broadly SE direction until the path joins the track that comes up from **Fuente Dé** (8.2km; 1390m). Follow this down to the car park.

WARNING. GPS is seriously affected by high walls. Ignore the readings on any device you are using both during the ascent and the descent. Use your mountain skills instead.

WALK 24
Peña Vieja

Start/Finish	El Cable (upper station)
Distance	11.8km
Ascent/Descent	1110m
Grade	Difficult
Time	6–7hr
Terrain	Steep, exposed and occasionally trackless during the ascent.
Map	Editorial Alpina; 1:25,000. Picos de Europa, Macizo Central y Oriental
Access	Follow the CA-185 to Fuente Dé from anywhere in the Liébana valley.
Parking	There is car parking all around the cable car complex. Arrive early for easy parking and access to the cable car. Tickets can be bought in advance at https://entradas.telefericofuentede.com.
Route finding	Easy except for the section above the Canal del Vidrio.

Peña Vieja is one of the most accessible and popular summits in the Picos de Europa. Most walkers tackle it directly from El Cable, the aptly named, upper cable car station. However, to add real flavour to the day, this circular walk approaches Peña Vieja via the Canal del Vidrio, a steep gully that cuts through the mountain's huge NE walls in unlikely positions. Doing this provides a superb circular tour of the Vieja Olvidada sub massif.

From El Cable (1850m), the upper station of the *teleférico*, follow **PR-PNPE 24** up the jeep track to the **Horcaína de Covarrobres** (1.2km; 1933m). Stay on the track and

Ascend the trackless slabs above the two tiny depressions

The Fuente del Resalau down off to the R is the last water on the route.

descend comfortably NE beneath the impressive SE walls of Peña Olvidada, but leave the track at a sharp R hairpin just above the **Chalet Real** (2.7km; 1760m). ◄ Contour round to gain and cross a **grassy spur** coming down from the E walls of Peña Vieja (3km; 1785m). The spur is a good place to map out the way ahead to the Canal del Vidrio, which lies due N. Also visible here are the remains of the **Minas de las Manforas** below to the NE.

The **Minas de las Manforas** were the most important mines in this part of the Picos de Europa. The Real Compañía Asturiana de Minas began prospecting for lead and zinc in 1853 and three years later started working the mines. The Manforas was worked fairly continuously until 1989. Mining at over 1500m created problems, and to resolve these the company built housing for both the engineers (the Chalet Real – see Walk 25) and the miners. Tracks were built to get the ore down to Espinama, and from there to

Unquera and onward transport. Part of the initial
treatment of the ore took place in the Canal del
Vidrio. The Canal owes its name to the glassy crys-
tals of galena, a lead ore that local shepherds collected as a supplement to their meagre earnings. The
'vidrio' (glass) was sold for ceramics manufacture in
Palencia, a city to the SE of the Picos.

From the col descend steeply to gain an old track.
This peters out to a path. Contour round on this and over
scree to gain the bottom of the **Canal del Vidrio** (3.9km;
1740m). Zig-zag up the centre of the gully on a loose,
poor path. Red paint dots help with the navigation – the
best route climbs diagonally to gain the L end of a narrow
natural rake that ascends R below mine entrances and an
old hut perched in an impressive position. ▸

When all seems lost the narrow path, heading S
by now, suddenly comes out onto a wide grassy ramp
(4.2km; 1830m). Follow a narrow zig-zag path N then
NW up the ramp. The way is marked by occasional green
paint dots that higher up revert to red. Trending off L, follow the vague path to two tiny *jous* (depressions). Ignore
a path off R. Instead move L to gain easy-angled slabs.
Ascend the trackless slabs WSW guided by small cairns.
An hour or so after exiting from the Canal del Vidrio you
should reach a small col due N of Peña Vieja (5.6km;
2375m). Due W lies the Collao de la Canalona, which
you go to on the descent. There are excellent views back
to the Eastern Massif, whilst the summit of Peña Vieja is
now clearly visible almost due S.

From the col follow a good path as it rises steadily
SW to join the standard ascent route in an airy position
above the steep SW walls of **Peña Vieja**. Follow the well-
trodden path up the final summit slope. An ice-axe and
even crampons may be necessary early in the season. The
summit is reached quite suddenly (6.4km; 2614m) and
provides stunning views in all directions.

The whole of the Central and Eastern massifs, and
a good part of the Western Massif, are visible from

The path cuts through
the headwalls of the
Canal del Vidrio in
spectacular positions,
with a long drop off R
into the main gully.

the summit of Peña Vieja. Peña Olvidada is visible in the near distance, and the dark double-headed summit of the Curavacas can be made out in the far distance out in the Cordillera Cantábrica, as can Peña Prieta and other major peaks in the range The village of Sotres is clearly visible to the NW, with the coast of Cantabria beyond.

Descend down the ascent route, but once above the steep SW walls of Peña Vieja, follow the main path round to the **Collao de la Canalona** (7.2km; 2451m). From the col drop W down the obvious gully, which is initially loose and needs care and patience. The descent path eventually joins PR-PNPE 23, the walk to and from Horcados Rojos (8km; 2020m). Follow **PR-PNPE 23** steeply down to the S (L) to reach the old miners' track at **La Vueltona**, a hairpin bend (9.4km; 1940m). Go L here and follow the jeep track as it contours SSE below the huge W walls of Peña Vieja and Peña Olvidada. On a hot day this section will be littered with the exhausted bodies of tourists who set out too late from El Cable and are wilting under the fierce afternoon sun. At the **Horcaína de Covarrobres** turn R and follow the track easily down to **El Cable** and the end of the route.

The figure largely responsible for the first systematic topographic survey of the three massifs of the Picos de Europa was the French mountaineer, the **Comte de Saint-Saud**. An expert on the Pyrenees, he arrived in the Picos by accident whilst holidaying with a friend from nearby Ribadesella. Such was his surprise on seeing the abruptness of the range, that he resolved to return to the area, and did so for the first time in 1890, when he made the first ascent of Peña Vieja.

WALK 25
Los Puertos de Áliva

Start	El Cable
Finish	Fuente Dé
Distance	13.9km
Ascent	280m
Descent	1070m
Grade	Moderate
Time	4–5hr
Terrain	Mostly on good tracks. One short, steep descent.
Map	Edición Alpina, 1:25,000. Picos de Europa, Macizos Central y Oriental.
Access	Follow the CA-185 to Fuente Dé from anywhere in the Liébana valley.
Parking	There is car parking all around the cable car complex. Arrive early for easy parking and access to the cable car. Tickets can be bought in advance at https://entradas.telefericofuentede.com.
Route finding	Easy. The route follows the waymarked PR-PNPE 24.

The Puertos de Áliva are extensive alpine pastures in grand surroundings and, as such, they have been silent witness to every kind of human activity associated with the Picos de Europa – hunting, farming, mining, climbing, and now tourism. The walk starts at El Cable, after the spectacular ride in the cable car from Fuente Dé, then climbs briefly to a highpoint at the Covarrobres col. After descending through open alpine meadows, the route suddenly changes character, crosses a rock garden and enters lush beech and oak forests on its way back to Fuente Dé.

From **El Cable** (1850m), the upper cable car station, follow the jeep track N to the **Horcaína de Covarrobres** col (1.2km; 1933m) at the foot of the impressive southern tip of **Peña Olvidada**. Follow the track comfortably down, initially beneath the towering walls that join Peña Olvidada to Peña Vieja, then past the **Chalet Real**, and so on to the **Hotel-Refugio de Áliva** (3.9km; 1665m).

The **Chalet Real** was constructed during the summer of 1912 by the Real Compañía de Asturias de Minas, who had won the rights to exploit the nearby Mina La Almanzora for zinc blend. The style of the building should feel familiar, since it was made from prefabricated sections brought directly from the England and was the first building of its type in Spain. Intended as a residence for the engineers working in the nearby mines, the Chalet Real boasted comforts such as running water, lighting, and central heating. Less intentional was that it should be used by King Alfonso XIII as a base for a hunting trip in September 1912.

Further down the hill are the green roofs of the **Hotel-Refugio de Áliva**, which was opened with due ceremony by Franco in 1966, at the same time as the cable car at Fuente Dé. The building replaced a small refuge that had been used by Alfonso XIII until the inauguration of the Chalet Real in 1912. Much more of a hotel than a refuge, both in services and prices, the Hotel-Refugio has been remodelled

From the Horcaína de Covarrobres the walk descends steadily into the Puertos de Áliva

The small chapel ahead is dedicated to the Virgen de la Salud, with a fiesta each year on the 2 July.

several times, and acts as a honey pot to tourists during the summer months.

Leave the hotel and turn R, following the track down to where the GR 202 comes in from the L from Sotres. ◄ Turn R and head S towards Espinama, with the summit of the Coriscao in the Cordillera Cantábrica suddenly filling the distant horizon. Cross a cattle grid, the **Portillas del Boquerón** (7.8km; 1350m) and, almost immediately afterwards, abandon the track to cross a small but sturdy wooden bridge over the **Río Nevandi**. The bridge leads to the start of a narrow path that is initially very steep but is also well trodden. This is the only difficult terrain on the whole route. The discomfort of the steep descent is mitigated in spring and early summer by the wealth of alpine rock plants and shrubby gorse the path passes through.

The narrow path ends suddenly at a track (8.3km; 1240m). Keeping an eye open for waymarking for PR-PNPE 24, follow the track into the mixed beech and oak woods that carpet this south-facing side of the valley. Avoid the temptation to drop down L at different moments along the track until you reach a fenced path that leads sharp R (NW) across a meadow (12km; 1080m). Follow this with very good views of Peña Remoña and the summits above Fuente Dé. Reach the meadow at the back of the Parador soon after, and the end of a relatively gentle, but varied walk.

WALK 26
Peña Oviedo

Start/Finish	Mogrovejo
Distance	10.8km
Ascent/Descent	720m
Grade	Moderate
Time	4hr
Terrain	Good tracks and paths.
Map	Editorial Alpina 1:25,000. Picos de Europa, Macizo Central y Oriental
Access	From Potes follow the CA-185 up through Camaleño. Just before Los Llanos, the CA-887 goes off R to Mogrovejo.
Parking	There is a car park to the NE of the village just after the church.
Route finding	Good waymarking throughout. The descent from the summit requires a little attention.

This pleasant circular walk starts and finishes in Mogrovejo, one of the most attractive villages in the Liébana valley. Perfect for an easier day, the route takes you to a summit that offers superb views of the SE walls of the Eastern Massif and the whole of the Upper Liébana valley. The walk is also a chance to discover some of the ancient and recent history of the area, from the Neolithic burial mounds near Peña Oviedo, to the abandoned village of Sebrango and the houses destroyed by the 2013 landslide.

From the car park walk back towards **Mogrovejo** and the church, then turn R and follow a jeep track up past the

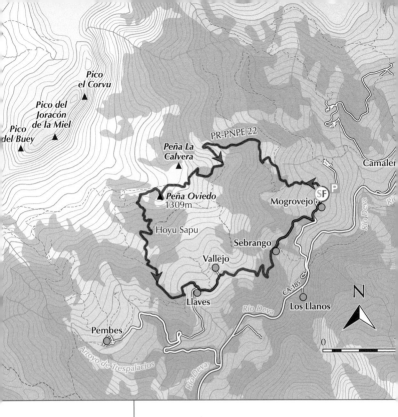

The Torre de Mogrovejo is from the 8th century, though the buildings surrounding it are from the 19th.

Museo de la Escuela (School Museum) and the Palacio de la Torre. ◄ After 800m the track divides. Take the R fork. At the next junction (1.1km; 780m), take the L fork, which is signposted **PR-PNPE 22** Peña Oviedo. Ascend amid woods and between meadows until the track swings L (2.6km; 1020m) and the angle eases. Continue up and go round to the W side of **Peña La Calavera** (*calavera* = skull).

A meadow off R after 3.6km offers excellent views NW to the Cumbre Avenas, and due N to the SE reaches of the Eastern Massif, especially the Picos de Cámara, Peña Cortés, the cube-like Morra de Lechugales, and the Silla Caballu (saddle).

Staying on the track, climb out of the woods onto the open ground of La Calavera, then leave the track to follow the obvious path to the summit of **Peña Oviedo** (4.5km; 1309m). The views are excellent in all directions: W to the Pico de Valdecoru; N to the Eastern Massif; E across the Liébana valley and S to Peña Prieta (the Dark Peak) in the main Cordillera Cantábrica.

Excavations done in and around Peña Oviedo and La Calavera between 1989 and 1991 reveal that there has been a human settlement in this area for over 5000 years. The settlers used fire to burn back the natural forest, which in those days would have been of oak, and create grazing land for their flocks of sheep and goats. In addition to various megalithic dolmens or funerary mounds, the excavations also revealed a walled terrace around Peña Oviedo. Nearby, archaeologists found traces of a circular pit some 90cm in diameter and 60cm deep, which was used as a silo for grain.

An old cubil *below Peña Oviedo*

From the summit descend to the main track but leave this immediately at the col going off L (SW) and descending on a wide grassy path. At a small clearing with a water trough, go down diagonally R to join a good track (5.1km; 1230m). Turn L and follow the track down among trees until you come quite suddenly to **Hoyu Sapu** and its two small, circular stone huts (*cubiles*) (5.5km; 1150m).

> The **two stone huts** are relatively recent. Neolithic settlers would have used wood and mud for their dwellings. Circular stone huts like these can be found all over the Picos and would normally have been for sheltering pigs.

From the huts follow the track through a gate, and at a junction some 200m later turn L and go down through oak and heavily coppiced hazel. Shortly after, the track enters the village of **Llaves**, you reach a T-junction (7.6km; 850m) and a drinking trough. Turn L here and walk out of the village and up past the church, with Pico Jano (Walk 20) dominating the view to the R. The scatter of houses that make up Vallejo soon appears to the L, but don't go up to them. Instead, drop down R (8.1km; 850m) on a track and that goes round below a telecommunications mast. Beyond the mast go steeply down on a little-used cobbled track until this swings sharp L and levels out to bring you to **Sebrango** (9.5km; 710m).

> In June 2013, one million cubic metres of earth and rocks forced some 40 villagers in Los Llanos and Sebrango to abandon their homes for fear of being buried in a landslide. A swathe of rock 300x300x10m threatens **Sebrango** to this day.

Leave Sebrango heading NE and follow the tarmac road back to sudden and re-assuring views of **Mogrovejo** and the end of the walk.

VALDEÓN

The Central Massif above Monte Corona and the Cares Gorge (Walk 32)

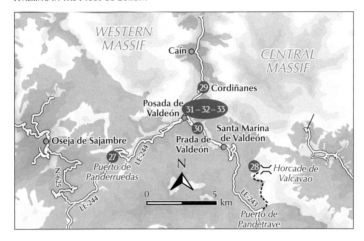

Valdeón is an ideal base for activities in the southern part of the Western and Central massifs and is the starting point for the Cares Gorge walk. Wilder and far more remote than the other valleys of the Picos, the effort needed to reach Valdeón is amply rewarded once there. The whole valley lies in the same rain shadow as the Liébana area, and consequently enjoys equally good weather, although the nights are cooler as most villages lie at altitudes around the 1000m mark. The scenery is epic: huge sweeps of pristine beech woods clothe the southern slopes of the valley, whilst kilometric walls of vertical rock close Valdeón to the north. In short, it's a mountaineer's paradise, with walks for all tastes and abilities.

Is there a downside to Valdeón? If there is, it is the limited services, with no bank or sizeable supermarket operating in the valley at the current time. This means you need to plan in terms of food and supplies before you get there, or shop in Riaño, some 45 minutes away by car. Accommodation, on the other hand, is more than adequate, and can be found in one form or another in all the villages in the valley. There is a campsite at Santa Marina de Valdeón, the highest village in the area. For details see https://campingelcares picosdeeuropa.com/en.

A new National Park visitor centre in Posada should, once it is open, provide the ideal way to get to grips with the rich history of Valdeón, but the real attraction when not out on the hills are the villages. There are excellent examples of traditional architecture in all of them. Especially attractive are the two- and four-slope grain stores known as *hórreos*. This

construction is strongly associated with Asturias, to the NW of the Picos de Europa, but is well represented in almost every village in Valdeón.

At the time of writing there are very limited bus services to Valdeón, so a car is obligatory. By car, the usual approach is from Cangas de Onís via the Desfiladero de los Beyos, Sajambre and the Puerto del Pontón (N-637). From Potes the approach is made via the Puerto de San Glorio (N-621), Portilla de la Reina, and the Puerto de Pandetrave. Scenically, both approaches have a huge amount to recommend them, despite the demands they place on the driver. There are various taxis services in Valdeón and these could be useful for getting to the start of some of the walks, or to visit Caín in the Cares Gorge. For details see https://valle devaldeon.es/en and search under 'Organize your trip'.

WALK 27
Pico Cebolleda

Start/Finish	Puerto de Panderruedas car park
Distance	13km
Ascent/Descent	770m
Grade	Difficult
Time	5–6hr
Terrain	Mostly good tracks and paths. Some very simple scrambling.
Map	Adrados Ediciones, 1:50,000. Parque Nacional de los Picos de Europa.
Access	The Puerto de Panderruedas is easily accessed along the LE-244 from Valdeón, and along the N-625 from Riaño or Oseja de Sajambre.
Parking	There is ample parking at Panderruedas.
Route finding	No waymarking. Trackless descent from the Collado de Cebolleda.

Several routes in this guide deliberately take you out of the Picos de Europa in order to reward you with better views of the main massifs. This walk not only offers superb views of the southern reaches of the Western and Central massifs and the start of the Cares Gorge, but also of the whole of the eastern section of the Cordillera Cantábrica. Not too long and not too strenuous, this is a good way to get your bearings for walking in this part of the Picos.

Leave the car park and picnic site (0km; 1460m) and cross the road. Pick up **PR-PNPE 11**, but branch off R immediately and go up a good jeep track, past a fountain and into beech woods. The track crosses a break in the trees that looks like a firebreak but is actually the result of running power lines underground, as is policy in the national Park whenever finance is available.

The track soon thins to a path. Follow this up, mostly to the R of the main crest of the spur, before coming out

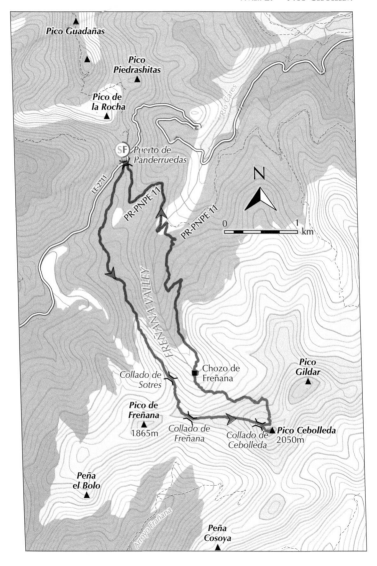

Pico Guadañas

Pico Piedrashitas

Pico de la Rocha

Río Cares

SF Puerto de Panderruedas

LE-2711

PR-PNPE 11

PR-PNPE 11

N

0   1
km

FREÑANA VALLEY

Collado de Sotres

Chozo de Freñana

Pico Gildar

Pico de Freñana
1865m

Collado de Freñana

Collado de Cebolleda

Pico Cebolleda
2050m

Peña el Bolo

Arroyo Freñana

Peña Cosoya

at a small clearing with magnificent views of Valdeón and the Picos de Europa to the N, and of the twin peaks of Ten and Pileñes to the S (2.4km; 1590m). Shortly after this, beech woods give way to rowan, and bilberries begin to carpet the ground.

When the tree cover recedes, you reach a broad ridge. This yields a bird's eye view of the Freñana valley, and a lone cabin sat in the cirque at the head of the valley. The south containing wall of the Freñana cirque is formed by the N face of the Pico Cebolleda, the high point of this walk, and the NW slopes of the Pico Gildar.

Take advantage of the view of the Freñana valley to work out the descent from the Pico Cebolleda to the lone cabin via the col just NW of the summit. Also take time to locate the start of the jeep track to the N of the hut as this is the descent you take later in the day.

About 1km along the ridge brings you to the **Collado de Sotres** (3.8km; 1735m) and the chance to escape E into Freñana. Ignore this, and climb quite steeply onto the ridge that climbs up to the **Collado de Freñana** (4.4km;

Climbing up to the Collado de Sotres

WALK 27 – PICO CEBOLLEDA

1830m). This provides sudden views of a multitude of Cordillera Cantábrica summits to the S. Swing E now and first follow the main ridge with some simple scrambling, and then a broader section that leads to the very shallow **Collado de Cebolleda** (5.4km; 1990m).

> The name **Cebolleda** (*cebolla* = onion) may be a reference to the heavily stratified rock visible in parts of the lower summit walls, and also on the rocks just below the summit itself. All the rock on this walk is quartzite and is substantially different to the limestone rock found in the main massifs of the Picos de Europa to the north.

Leave your rucksacks at the Collado de Cebolleda if you wish, and make the final, short ascent to the summit of the **Pico Cebolleda** (2050m) by way of some simple scrambling. Revel in some of the best all-round views anywhere in Northern Spain, but try to pick out the Torre Salinas (Walk 28), the Torre Bermeja (Walk 32), and the Cares Gorge (Walk 33).

Return to the col, then, descending first E and then N, make your way down into the upper cirque of the **Freñana valley**. Next work essentially W across track-less ground (occasional small cairns), with the Collado de Sotres as a general guide to the W. Finally swing N and descend more steeply to the lone cabin you spotted earlier in the day, the **Chozo de Freñana** (7.9km; 1610m).

> Several streams converge around the hut in Freñana. Although they appear innocent enough, they are, in fact, the source of the **River Cares**. Lower down, these innocent waters have their way through well over 1000m of solid limestone to carve out the setting for one of the most spectacular walks in Spain, the Cares Gorge (Walk 33).

After a short descent N pick up a well-used jeep track and follow this into beech woods and welcome shade if the weather is at all hot. ▶ Follow the track down through

There is a magical quality to these immense woods as the sunlight filters through the leaf canopy in spring, summer and autumn.

the woods until it joins the jeep track taken by **PR-PNPE 11** (10.9km; 1365m). Turn L and go over the **River Cares**, still no more than a busy stream, then round a broad spur, and finally up to the car park at **Panderruedas**, and the end of a perfect introduction to this sector of the Picos de Europa.

WALK 28
La Torre Salinas

Start/Finish	Horcada de Valcavao
Distance	8.6km
Ascent/Descent	820m
Grade	Difficult
Time	5hr
Terrain	A good track to start and finish, but quite often steep and exposed during the ascent and descent. Some simple scrambling.
Map	Editorial Alpina, 1:25,000. Picos de Europa, Macizo Central y Oriental. Adrados Ediciones, 1:50,000. Parque Nacional de los Picos de Europa
Access	Head SE from Valdeón on the LE-2703 to the Puerto de Pandetrave. Once at Pandetrave, follow the jeep track that branches off NE to the parking space at the Horcada de Valcavao. (It is possible to walk from Pandetrave but allow an extra 3hr in total.)
Route finding	Easy to and from the Canal de Pedabejo. Trackless over the central section.

Valdeón is dominated to the E by a series of summits which together form the Peñas de Cifuentes. The Torre Salinas, whilst not the highest nor the most spectacular, is one of the most significant. The first ascent in 1853 heralded the beginning of alpinism in the Picos de Europa. Today, as then, it offers magnificent views of large sections Central and Western Massifs, and of much of Valdeón and the Cordillera Cantábrica.

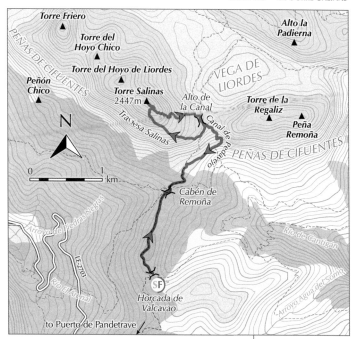

From the fenced car park at the **Horcada de Valcavao**, follow the jeep track N to the **Cabén de Remoña** (1.3km; 1780m). Reaching the Cabén de Remoña brings you onto the Ediciones Alpina map and to the end of the track. Follow the waymarked path past cattle pens and across beneath the walls of the **Peñas de Cifuentes** and then down to the entrance to the **Canal de Pedavejo** (2.4km; 1790m).

Work up the stony gully, first on the R below the Torre de la Regaliz, and then further L on a better path. Just before reaching the Alto de la Canal, a small path branches S past a large boulder (3km; 2025m). Ignore the yellow and white cross on the boulder and follow the tiny path up and round SW to gain access to the **Traviesa Salinas**, the grassy slopes that cut across the whole of the

179

central section of the S walls of the Torre Salinas. Where the path begins to descend steeply into a rocky gully, abandon it and take to the trackless ground that leads W across steep grassy slopes, staying fairly close to the walls above.

The maps show the summit of the Torre Salinas as 2447m, but the summit cairn shows the figure 2430m. Who cares!

A vague path appears from time to time during the traverse, which crosses a number of shoulders, each higher than the last. Eventually, the grass gives way to rocky ground. Work across this until it becomes feasible to climb N up broken ground and then NE to the summit ridge (4.3km; 2410m). Scramble along W to the **Torre Salinas** summit itself (2447m). ◄

The summit views are magnificent. Collado Jermoso and the Torre de Llambrión fill the sky to the north. Peña Vieja lies to the NE, the upper cable car station to the E, and most of the Western Massif can been seen to the W. Valdeón lies at your feet and over 300km of the Cordillera Cantábrica stretch out from SE to SW.

On the summit with the Torre de Llambrión in the background

You can either descend by the ascent route or, for a more varied and more testing day, scramble ESE along and down the summit ridge (small cairns) to a point at which the cairns lead steeply down L and into a short,

stony gully. Descend into the gully and scramble down it. This seems easiest by staying close to the R wall following the many small cairns. Leave the gully heading out R (SE) and then cross back L (NE) and work E across some steep terrain until this levels out and slabby ground leads to the **Alto de la Canal** (1.1km from summit; 2035m). ▸

From the Alto de la Canal descend to the **Cabén de Remoña** and from there follow the track back to the **Horcada de Valcavao**, though not without stopping from time to time to turn and enjoy the views of the day's achievements.

This descent is actually the Normal Route and is an alternative to going across the exposed grassy slopes of the Traviesa Salinas.

CASIANO DE PRADO

Whilst early ascents in the Picos were done by shepherds going about their business, the beginning of climbing is generally accredited to the Spanish geologist and mining engineer, Casiano de Prado. Working in the Cordillera Cantábrica between Palencia and León, he first spotted the Picos in 1845. His first visit to the range was to no avail because of bad weather, but he returned two years later, and made the first ascent of the Torre Salinas on 28 July 1853, in the company of two French colleagues.

Once on the summit, De Prado used a mercury barometer to measure the height. Their calculations gave a result of 2500m, which we now know to be wrong. But also incorrect was the information that De Prado had been given in Portilla de la Reina, where the local people had said that the Torre Salinas was the highest summit in the Picos. The view from the top immediately revealed that the Torre de Llambrión to the north was higher, and this was confirmed later that day by the Mayor of Prada de Valdeón. This left De Prado with no choice but to return in 1856. The sport of climbing had arrived in the Picos de Europa.

WALK 29
Collado Jermoso

Start/Finish	Car park, Cordiñanes
Distance	14.3km
Ascent/Descent	1765m
Grade	Very difficult
Time	8–10hr
Terrain	Poor paths in places. Steep, exposed and potentially dangerous at different points.
Map	Editorial Alpina, 1:25,000. Picos de Europa, Macizo Central y Oriental
Access	Cordiñanes lies 2.5km N of Posada de Valdeón on the road to Caín. The car park for Collado Jermoso lies above the village to the NW among trees.
Route finding	Mostly straightforward; the fierce terrain leaves no options.

Even though this is the approach route to the Jermoso hut, it is a serious high-mountain walk, especially early in the season when late snow can make an ice-axe and crampons obligatory. The walk should not be undertaken by anyone with a fear of heights as the path is narrow, airy and exposed in a number of places. However, Collado Jermoso is every bit as beautiful as its name suggests (*jermoso* = beautiful) and the hut provides water, refreshment and security after the first half of the walk. The views get better as the day goes on, and Asotín in the afternoon is quite different to the same place earlier in the day.

Leave the car park (0km; 860m) heading NE on an old track. After some 300m leave the track on a path that climbs steeply R to the walls beneath the **Peña del Porracho**. Ignore any GPS data from now until you reach Jermoso. The high walls make it wholly unreliable.

A path cut into the sheer rock face leads out N to a shoulder on the Porracho spur. From here follow the path

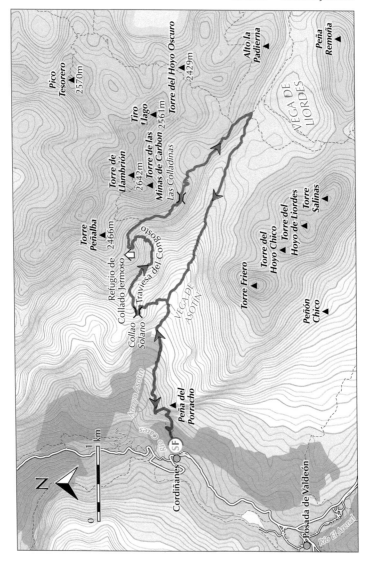

183

E, at times in airy positions, as it engineers its way across more vertical walls. The path is known as the Senda de la Rienda. The beech woods are a welcome haven after the exposed position of the path but take care not to lose your way here. Leave the woods and climb quite steeply up to the first piece of level ground since leaving the car park. This is the **Vega l'Asotín** (2.7km; 1400m) and is a great place for breakfast. ◄

Leave Asotín heading N and occasionally W on a loose but well-used path. The hard work ends at the small but delightful **Collao Solano** (3.4km; 1620m), which provides stunning views of the Western Massíf and the upper Cares Gorge. ◄

Leave Solano on a narrow path and follow this up and along the **Traviesa del Congosto** in exposed positions. Late snow can make this section dangerous. A high point is reached opposite and almost due N of the Torre Friero (4.4km; 1840m), whose deep gullies and sharp crests are clearly visible. Now descend and gain the base of the steep, narrow, rocky gully that comes down from Jermoso. This is the Argayo Congosto, and it may have snow until mid season. Only enter the gully if you are

The Asotín beech woods were declared a World Heritage Site by UNESCO in 2017.

If you have not been comfortable on the walk so far, turn back now. What lies ahead is harder.

The Jermoso hut with the Torre Salinas behind and Las Colladinas top left

confident about the terrain and the conditions. The best path in the upper section lies to the R of the gully bed, but everything is quite steep and loose. The **Jermoso hut** becomes visible off L on leaving the gully and is easily reached along a good path (5.2km; 2046m). ▶ **Collado Jermoso** itself offers unbeatable views SW over the whole of Valdeón and W across to the Western Massif. Because of the views, many walkers stay overnight at the hut to enjoy the sunset. There is a lot to recommend this and tackling the Torre Salinas from Liordes the following day (see Walk 28). However, in summer book ahead to guarantee your place.

The Jermoso hut is also known as the Refugio Diego Mella. Mella was the driving force behind the Peñalba mountaineering club in the city of León.

Leave the hut heading E and skirting around the head of the Argayo Congosto. A good path climbs to **Las Colladinas** (6.7km; 2180m), a grassy shoulder to the S of the **Torre de las Minas de Carbón**. This section can also be badly affected by late snow. Descend from the col and cross easier ground to where a sign indicates the Colladina de las Nieves off L (Walk 22). Ignore this and descend R in exposed positions on a narrow path that leads down to the N edge of the delightful **Vega de Liordes** (8.5km; 2000m; Walk 21).

Swing W now and follow an ill-defined path over initially comfortable ground. The path soon improves but the terrain steepens and becomes a dry, stony gully. Go down this staying mostly on the R at first, and passing beneath the huge Torre Friero gullies and walls. The path levels off and enters the **Vega l'Asotín** (11.6km; 1400m), and the end of the day's difficulties.

Reverse the morning's approach to Asotín back down through the woods and along the narrow path around the **Peña del Porracho**. The shoulder provides a sudden, bird's eye view of **Cordiñanes**. Follow the path as it descends below the Perracho walls, and then continue on down to the car park (14.3km, 880m).

WALK 30
El Valle del Arenal

Start/Finish	Prada de Valdeón, 50m SE of village at bridge over Río Arenal
Distance	12.6km
Ascent/Descent	825m
Grade	Moderate
Time	4–5hr
Terrain	Mostly tracks and good paths.
Map	Adrados Ediciones, 1:50,000. Parque Nacional de los Picos de Europa
Access	From Posada de Valdeón via the LE-243. Parking is possible at the bridge that marks the start of the PR-PNPE 14, but is probably best on the LE-243 at the junction with the lane to Prada.
Route finding	Straightforward except for two short sections.

This is a walk of two contrasting halves connecting two very attractive villages. The first half follows the old livestock trail that linked Valdeón to the Liébana valley in times gone by. The route is open and offers superb views of the whole area. The second half takes you into the immense beech woods that clothe the southern reaches of Valdeón and are one of the gems of the national park. These are a joy at any time of the year.

The route starts and finishes in **Prada de Valdeón**, near a small bridge over the **Río El Arenal** just S of the village (960m). This marks the start of PR-PNPE 14, and is the place where this walk finishes. Some 50m to the NW, locate the start of **PR-PNPE 15**, the Senda del Mercadillo, and from there follow a lane N past an attractive *hórreo*, then skirt up and around a house to reach an underpass below the **LE-2703**. Coming out from the underpass, head N and join a track that climbs steadily but pleasantly up and round the W side of predominantly oak-covered slopes.

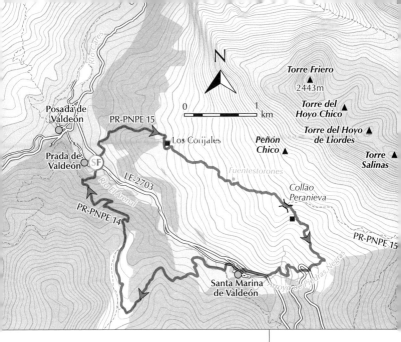

The outskirts of Prada and the start of the walk

The route away from Prada follows tracks and paths that were used traditionally by farmers from Valdeón in order to take their livestock over to the markets in the neighbouring valley of Liébana. Similar paths and tracks were used by farmers from Santa Marina de Valdeón, also taking their livestock to Liébana. These two groups of trails, known as the **Sendas del Mercadillo**, met at the Cabén de Remoña (Walk 28) before descending to Fuente Dé and accessing the markets (*mercados*) in the Camaleño district of the Liébana valley.

The woods recede, open ground is reached (1.4km; 1145m), and the view to the L is dominated by the southern walls of the Central Massif. Soon after, a broad shoulder by a walled field offers superb views S to the endless beech woods of the southern reaches of Valdeón, and W to the Torre Bermeja group (Walk 32). Almost immediately after this you come to the hut at **Los Corijales** (1.8km; 1200m). The best path lies just beyond the hut to the NE where the track dies out. Here animal tracks all head SE up over heathery slopes. Eventually you reach a small but prominent cabin, just beyond which is a drinking trough. This is **Fuentestorones** (3.2km; 1440m).

Leave Fuentestorones heading E and steadily gaining height until you reach a broad grassy col by two rocky outcrops. The **Collao Peranieva** is the high point of the route (4km; 1580m).

It's worth climbing up onto the **rocky outcrops** to the SW for the views around the whole of the Arenal valley, as well as the surrounding mountains. They are also a good place to study the sides of the valley. The slopes to the south of the river are north facing, shady and humid and so are covered in dense beech forest. The south-facing drier slopes of the N side of the valley are almost treeless and are covered in brackens, gorse and heathers. The differences in rock type and forms are also notable. The jagged, pale grey limestones of the Picos dominate the view to the W and N, whilst the gentler, more rounded skyline to the south is made from the siliceous rocks of the Cordillera Cantábrica.

At the col abandon PR-PNPE 15 and descend SE past the **lone cabin** at Urdias and then across a small stream. Continue down SE until it is possible to swing SW and descend to the Pandetrave road and signs for PR-PNPE 15 (5.5km; 1370m). Cross the road just E of a wide hairpin and descend to **Santa Marina**, arriving at the village bus stop. Turn R and follow the **LE 2703** W staying above the village. At a lookout point with information boards walk down into the village (6.8km; 1165m).

Santa Marina, the highest village in Valdeón, had its own Junta Vecinal (neighbourhood council) until the 19th century. Independent in more than just its geographical position, it is also the oldest village in Valdeón, and conserves good examples of local architecture, including 12 superb *hórreos*.

An hórreo with a two-slope roof in Santa Marina

From the village descend W on a good track to the river. Cross this and immediately turn R on the **PR-PNPE 14** to Prada. The track soon enters the beech woods we admired during the morning from the Collao Peranieva. After some 2km a waymarked track goes off L (9.6km; 1260m). This is an optional part of the PR-PNPE 14 that goes up to the pastures at Montó but it is probably best left for another day. ◄

Though beech dominates these woods, look out for hazel, cherry and hawthorn at the edges of any clearings.

Staying on the main track, enjoy the superb views R across to the Central Massif and a large part of the morning's walk, and NW to the Bermeja group on the southern edge of the Western Massif (Walk 32). The hard work is over, and it only now remains to follow the PR-PNPE 14 and amble down to **Prada**. The track reaches the village at the bridge over the **Río Arenal**.

WALK 31
Pueblos de Valdeón

Start/Finish	Town Hall (Ayuntamiento) in Posada de Valdeón.
Distance	7.8km
Ascent/Descent	360m
Grade	Easy
Time	3hr
Terrain	Good tracks and paths throughout.
Map	Adrados Ediciones, 1:50,000. Parque Nacional de los Picos de Europa
Access	Easy from anywhere in Valdeón along the LE-243, or from Sajambre via the N-625 to the Puerto del Pontón, and then the LE-244.
Route finding	Straightforward. Well signed. The walk follows the PR-PNPE 11 over the first third and the PR-PNPE 12 from Caldevilla onwards.

This walk takes you up into the extensive beech woods that covers the SW corner of Valdeón, and then leads you back to Posada through the neat, tidy villages of Caldevilla and Soto. Both are rich in examples of local architecture, and the contrast between the woodland and the villages makes this an interesting walk that is best undertaken in the afternoon, when the sun on the surrounding mountains is a spectacle of light and colour.

From the Town Hall (920m) cross the road and pick up the **PR-PNPE 11** as it climbs SW away from the town, swinging around the old National Park visitor centre en route (0.3km; 950m). A signpost for the Mirador de la Cruz appears (0.7km; 1010m), and you might want to make a short excursion to the lookout point and its views over central Valdeón.

The track climbs steadily away from **Posada** through mature oak and beech woodland. Ignore a track off L (1.6km; 1110m) and climb on to where the trees recede for a moment, and the track swings SE and levels out (2km; 1180m). ▸

Stay on the track as it works its way around the upper reaches of the **Riega de Pamporquera** and then begins a gentle descent to the **Arroyo de Arriba**. Leave

Woodland like this is magnificent at any time of the year, but especially in the late autumn.

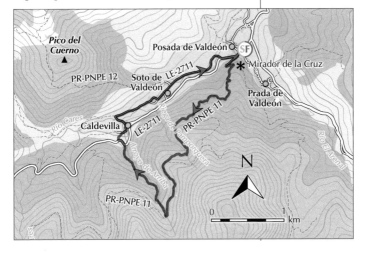

The track levels out and works its way around the Riega Riegade Pamporquera

the PR-PNPE 11 at this point (3.7km; 1220m; signed Caldevilla) and turn right to drop down NW on a good path. Descend through the woods, first on the R bank of the stream and then on the L. The path comes out at a wide curve on the LE-2711 road (5km; 1020m). Turn L, go up the road 120m and drop down R on a muddy track that ends in **Caldevilla**.

Despite its diminuitive size, Caldevilla has its own village hall (**Casa del pueblo**). This is a simple, two-storey structure. The upper floor has large openings where hay was passed into the barn in order to feed the village bull, who originally lived below.

Walk down through the village and cross the **River Cares** to pick up the **PR-PNPE 12**, which leads NE to

Soto de Valdeón. Go past the 11th-century Iglesia de San Pedro and take the L fork soon after at a junction in the village (6.1km; 965m). ▸

As you wander around Caldevilla and Soto, in addition to *hórreos*, look out for springs (*fuentes*), drinking troughs (*abrevaderos*) and watermills (*molinos*). You might also admire the first-floor balconies of the most traditional houses. There are excellent views of the Central Massif from Caldevilla all the way back to Posada.

On leaving Soto the road becomes a track. Follow this to its junction with the LE-244 (7.5km; 930m). Turn L and walk along the LE-244 and back into **Posada de Valdeón**.

The San Pedro ad Víncula fiesta on 1 August is one of the best in the valley.

HÓRREOS

One unique element of the villages of the Picos de Europa in Asturias and León are the *hórreos*, the wooden grain stores that stand on stilts in order to protect the harvest and other foods from the damp and, more importantly, from rodents.

No two *hórreos* are the same, and it is worth wandering around the villages to make comparisons. But perhaps the most curious thing about the *hórreos* in the villages of Valdeón is that they show two different structures, with either two- or four-slope roofs.

All *hórreos* stand on wood or stone stilts (*pegollos*) topped with large, flat wood or stone plates (*tornarratas*). These plates make it impossible for vermin to climb into the hórreo. The granary itself is built up from four huge beams (*los rabes*) that interlock at the corners. The ends of the beams in Valdeón are decorated in a range of different ways.

See also: https://valledevaldeon.es/en and search under discover the valley heritage.

WALK 32

La Travesona

Start/Finish	Posada de Valdeón
Distance	15km (+ 2km for the Torre Bermeja option)
Ascent/Descent	1230m (+ 400m for the Torre Bermeja option)
Grade	Very difficult
Time	7–9hr (+ 2–3hr for the Torre Bermeja option)
Terrain	Tracks and good paths for the start and finish. Some steep, indefinite paths over the central section, though with small cairns most of the way.
Map	Editorial Alpina, 1:25,000. Picos de Europa, Macizo Occidental
Access	The walk starts in the main square in Posada de Valdeón, which can be accessed easily from anywhere in Valdeón, or from Sajambre via the Puerto del Pontón.
Parking	Many places around the main square.

A varied, complete and really satisfying circular walk that takes you into high-mountain scenery, but always with Valdeón and the Central Massif as the backdrop. The sudden, spectacular and wide-ranging views from the Collao Verde will be the highlight of the day for many, but there is barely a moment that does not feel good. Navigation down from the Collao Verde and along the Traversona needs to be spot on, especially at the beginning, but the situation is wonderful.

From the main square in **Posada** (920m) walk past Casa Abascal and then W over the **River Cares**. Turn L immediately after crossing the river and follow a track comfortably up until a well-kept **cabin** appears on the R (1.9km; 1125m). At this point, the roof and chimney of a **second cabin** are visible a little higher up, and you can see a third cabin higher up still to the N on the edge of a spur overlooking Valdeón. Leave the track and follow the small cairns that go off R and mark the start of a path. Follow

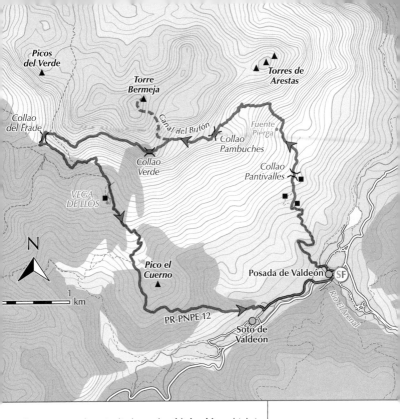

the narrow path as it climbs to the **third cabin**, which is actually on the **Collao Pantivalles** (2.4km; 1255m).

Cross the Pantivalles col heading N and descend slightly at first, then work up through the edge of woodland to reach the **Fuente Piergua** (3km; 1330m), and the last of the last water until the Vega de Llós on the descent. From the drinking trough follow the path until it leaves the woods. Ignore a small, cairned path that descends off R and crosses the slopes to the N. Instead climb up to gain the obvious scree cone that comes down from the imposing walls of the **Torres de Arestas**. The narrowest part of the scree is best taken on the R on a steep path with occasional small cairns.

The Bermeja group from the Caben de Remoña (as viewed from Walk 28)

The last section up to Pambuches is on grass, which in the late spring is a garden of yellow gentians. This is also a good place to spot rebecos.

When you approach the top of the scree cone, cross over W and begin to work laboriously up the L side of a boulder field following a narrow but well-cairned path that leads up to the Collao Pambuches (5.1km; 1885m). ◄ The high point of the route, the **Collao Verde** is evident above and almost due W of the Pambuches col. Also evident is the large scree cone that comes down from the **Canal del Bufón**, the upper section of the normal route from Valdeón to the Torre Bermeja (2392m) from Valdeón.

TORRE BERMEJA ASCENT

For the ascent of the Torre Bermeja, go up the steep Canal del Bufón screes, mainly on the R below the walls of El Bolo (2166m). Once level with the Bolo summit, continue among large blocks with small cairns and a vague path, until it is possible to work up and out L (W) to gain the col due S of the Bermeja. Go around the south walls of the Bermeja on a well-used path to gain the summit. The descent is by the same route. Allow a full 3hr extra if you decide to go for the Torre Bermeja summit, and consider returning to Posada by the morning's ascent route.

From the Pambuches col cairns, follow a narrow path over rough stony terrain to the base of the scree from the Canal del Bufón. Rather than be tempted R up the scree as per the Alpina map, stay L and work directly up to the **Collao Verde** (6km; 2083m). It will seem like hard work, but the reward is the sudden, stunning view of most of the Cordillera Cantábrica and many mountains in Eastern Asturias.

Visible to the W and NW are Pica Beza (Walk 34) and Pico Jario (Walk 36 above Soto de Sajambre, as well as the Upper Dobra valley (Walk 9). The Pico Cebolleda (Walk 27) can be seen to the S, while the Torre Salinas (Walk 28) and Collado Jermoso (Walk 29) lie to the NE.

From the Collao Verde scan the route ahead to the W. The ground below the walls of the Torre del Collao Verde is split by three grassy slopes. This route takes the middle of the three. To get there, descend SW over steep grass from the Collao Verde then swing NW and traverse on a poor path at the foot of steep walls. Climb up briefly to a small col with cairns (6.4km; 2025m), then descend on a better path, though still narrow and rocky in places. Do not attempt to go straight down from the Collao Verde

On the screes just before reaching the Collao Verde

The Collao del Frade is another place where the chances of seeing rebecos are good.

or from any point on this path. Despite the good views of the Vega de Llós below, safe descent is not possible. When the middle grass terrace is finally reached, the Collao del Frade is evident below. ◄ Contour round W then descend steeply over shaley ground to reach the col (8.1km; 1790m).

Take the higher of the two paths that go SE from the **Collao del Frade** and contour round above walls until a broken path zig-zags down to the drinking trough in the **Vega de Llós** (9.6km; 1590m). From the far side of the *vega* pick up waymarking for the **PR-PNPE 12**. Go down through beech woods to a second spring and trough. The track divides here (11km; 1340m), with the L option signed to Posada de Valdeón. This becomes a path down through oak woods and ends in the upper part of Soto de Valdeón. Go L round the attractive Casa Vieja hotel, and pick up the old road to **Posada**, which you reach next to the new National Park visitor centre.

The Vega de Llós is typical of the middle-mountain pastures that have been so important to **livestock farming** for so long in the Picos de Europa. Cattle were brought up here in the late spring and left to feed on the lush grass until the end of the summer. Today there are times when there are as many *rebecos* as cows, which is a joy to behold as a visitor to the area, but less so for local farmers, as it signifies the death of a centuries-old practice. Moreover, most of the cows you are likely to see in Llós today are there to produce beef. In fact, according to one of the locals in Santa Marina, in 2019 there were no longer any dairy cattle in Valdeón, forcing local cheese producers to import milk from elsewhere.

WALK 33

The Cares Gorge

Start	Posada de Valdeón
Finish	Poncebos
Distance	20km
Ascent	160m
Descent	900m
Grade	Moderate
Time	5–7hr
Terrain	Tracks and a good but narrow and very exposed path. Do not attempt the gorge if you suffer from vertigo.
Map	Editorial Alpina, 1:25,000. Picos de Europa, Macizos Occidental, Central y Oriental
Access	The walk starts in the main square in Posada de Valdeón. During the peak summer season, from mid-July to mid-August, ALSA (Appendix A) run buses from Cangas de Onís to Posada de Valdeón, and from Poncebos back to Cangas de Onís. This is the easiest way to walk the whole route and get back to the start on the same day. Alternatively, you could walk from Caín to Poncebos and then back, or vice versa. Either option is 24km and takes about 6hr.
Route finding	The walk follows PR-PNPE 3 throughout. Ignore GPX tracking. High walls and poor reception make it meaningless.

This is possibly the most famous walk in Spain and the summer sees big numbers of people on the path, especially near Poncebos and Caín. But the Cares Gorge is truly spectacular, particularly the section between these two villages, and it is well worth sharing with other walkers, even on a busy day. Walls, crags and stunning rock towers rise up over 2000m in places, while over the section immediately after Caín the gorge is only a few metres wide. Cloudy, overcast days are just as impressive as sunny ones, if not better, making this a good poor-weather outing.

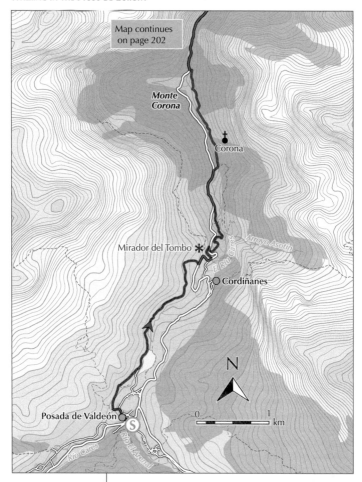

Map continues on page 202

Monte Corona

✝ Corona

Mirador del Tombo ✳

El Río Cares   Arroyo Asotín

○ Cordiñanes

N

0   1
km

Posada de Valdeón ○
Ⓢ

Río Cares   Río El Arenal

From the main square in Posada (0km; 920m) walk past Casa Abascal and then W over the **River Cares**. Turn R after crossing the river and follow a good track N and then NE amid hay meadows on the L bank of the River Cares. There are good views of the tiny hamlet of **Cordiñanes** off

R and then the paths drops down to reach the **Mirador del Tombo** (3.3km; 820m)

> The **Mirador del Tombo** was built in memory of Don Julián Delgado Úbeda, at one time the President of the Spanish Mountaineering Federation. Apart from the statue of a *rebeco*, the chamois found throughout the Pico de Europa, the viewing platform has a panel that allows you to identify the summits that tower over you to the N in both the Western and Central massifs.

Take the path that sets off from behind the panel, drop down and cross the road to Caín, follow the path past the Barrejo bridge and come out again on the road. Stay on the road for some 500m then drop down R, cross the Cares and reach the chapel at **Corona** (5.3km; 630m). ▸

Follow the path along the R bank of the river until it joins the road once more. Follow the road, which can be busy in the summer, until it ends in the tiny village of **Caín**, with its bars and restaurants (9km; 460m).

Tradition has it that the Asturian nobleman Pelayo was crowned (corona = crown) here prior to the Battle of Covadonga in 718 AD.

The tunnels just after Caín

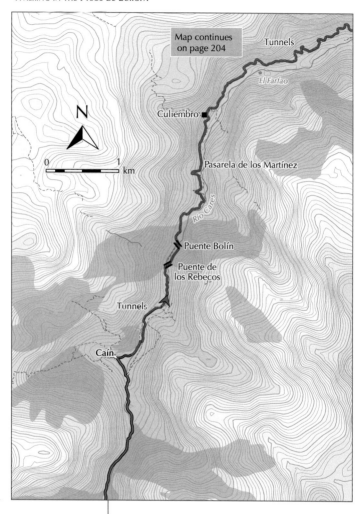

Map continues
on page 204

Tunnels

El Farfao

Culiembro

Pasarela de los Martínez

Rio Cares

Puente Bolín

Puente de
los Rebecos

Tunnels

Caín

Caín is the birthplace of the shepherd who accompanied the Marquis of Villaviciosa on the historic first ascent of El Naranjo de Bulnes in 1904. El

Cainejo, whose real name was Gregorio Pérez, was well used to scrambling barefoot up and down formidably steep rocks and walls – that was just part of his job. A plaque in the upper part of the village marks the house where Pérez was born and lived.

Leave Caín heading N on the L bank of the river, cross the river and then cross back at a small dam and go through a sequence of short **tunnels** that allow just enough light in to make torches unnecessary. The gorge opens out briefly after the tunnels, then closes in again at the **Puente de los Rebecos**, where it crosses over the river to the R bank. Shortly after it crosses back at the **Puente Bolín** (11km; 420m) where there is a spring with drinking water. This whole section is especially spectacular; the gorge is at its narrowest and the sky is reduced to a thin strip of blue or grey above your head.

The **path from Caín to Poncebos** was cut into the often-vertical rock walls between 1945 and 1950 to provide access for labourers working on the maintenance of the channel that carries water from Caín to the hydroelectric power station at Poncebos. The channel itself was built between 1915 and 1921 and involved boring 71 tunnels by hand.

The Pasarela de los Martínez, an artificial walkway built in 2012 after the wall of the gorge collapsed, taking with it a section of the 1945 path. Named after Alfonso and Juan Tomás Martínez, two brothers from Camarmeña whose lives were dedicated to the Picos de Europa and El Naranjo de Bulnes, the floor of the walkway allows you to stare down precipitously to the river below.

Not long after crossing the Bolín bridge the path comes to the **Pasarela de los Martínez**. Shortly after, you reach old shepherds' cabins at **Culiembro** (13.5km; 440m), the halfway point of the Garganta Divina, the name given to the section of the Cares Gorge from Caín to Poncebos.

CARES GORGE GEOLOGY

The geology of the Cares Gorge is well worth studying during the walk. The Hercynian and Alpine orogenies created the fracture that the Cares now runs through, but its current shape is the product of first glaciation and then fluvial erosion. The glaciers in the Picos came down to 600m above sea level and left the gorge with the classic U-shaped profile. But the erosion of the river water running over the porous limestone rock created a classic V-shaped cut in the floor of the glacial 'U'. This is clearly visible from the path as you look east during the approach to Los Collaos. Also visible from time to time during the walk are surgencies, which are natural springs that emerge suddenly from the solid rock. The first of these is visible in the spring or after heavy rain just before reaching Caín. The most spectacular is El Farfao on the opposite side to the path after 14.5km. The water of these springs has come down from summits in excess of 2000m in the Central and Western massifs.

As you move on from Culiembro and through a number of short tunnels, the gorge begins to open out and slowly swing 90 degrees to end up heading east. This section ends with a short climb up to the high point of the gorge at **Los Collaos** (17.6km; 520m). From here follow the path as it descends steadily to where it finally drops down quite suddenly to the jeep track that leads to **Poncebos**. Turn L and amble down to join the throng of happy walkers in the bars at the end of the walk (20km; 260m).

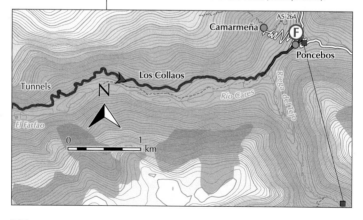

SAJAMBRE

Peña Santa de Castilla from the Pica Beza (Walk 34)

Sajambre is the smallest sector in the guide, but what it lacks in size it makes up for in other ways. The villages cluster around Oseja, the capital, and are surrounded by ancient beech woods and sheer rock walls. The walks range from strolls along centuries-old drove roads, to long days in middle- and high-mountain terrain. Walk 35 takes you to the foot of the vast south face of Peña Santa de Castilla in the heart of the Western Massif. In contrast, Walk 37 takes through idyllic woods and tiny villages.

Oseja de Sajambre has enough basic services to make a short stay comfortable, with a small supermarket, a chemist's and three bars, two of which have basic restaurant services. In such a small place, accommodation is limited, although there are several rural houses for rent in both Oseja and Soto. There is no campsite and the nearest petrol stations are some way away in Riaño or Cangas de Onís.

The national park has recently opened a visitor centre in the heart of Oseja. The displays provide an excellent introduction to the geology, landscape, flora and fauna of the Picos de Europa. They are well worth a visit even if you do not intend to walk in the Sajambre sector, since the information is well presented and valid for the range as a whole. For more details go to www.turismocastillayleon.com/en and search for "La Fonseya Information Center".

As with the Valdeón sector, Sajambre is best visited using private transport, and is reached from Cangas de Onís along the N-625, or from Riaño along the same road via the Puerto del Pontón. Both approaches are memorable, although for quite different reasons. There is an infrequent bus service between Oseja de Sajambre and Cangas de Onís. Up-to-date details can be found at: www.alsa.com/en/web/bus/home A 24-hour taxi service can be contacted by telephone at 630 322 243.

WALK 34

Pica Beza

Start/Finish	Soto de Sajambre car park (910m)
Distance	13.9km
Ascent/Descent	1130m
Grade	Difficult
Time	6–8hr
Terrain	Good tracks and paths except for the ascent of Pica Beza from the Collada de Beza.
Map	Editorial Alpina, 1:25,000. Picos de Europa, Macizo Occidental
Access	Take the N625 to just S of Oseja de Sajambre. For four hair-raising kilometres follow the largely single-track road to Soto. The car park is signposted off L just before reaching Soto.
Route finding	Well signed except for the ascent to Pica Beza.

Peña Beza totally dominates the view north from Soto de Sajambre, its huge rock walls seeming impenetrable. Thankfully this is not the case and a hidden gully with some simple scrambling provides the key to the ascent. Pica Beza, the highest of the Peña Beza summits, offers abundant rewards to any who have made the effort, with outstanding views in all directions. Add to this the descent through Los Llerones, and you have one of the best walks in the area.

From the car park walk through **Soto de Sajambre** (0km; 910m), going past the old school and the church. Just before the road goes R over the **Agüera river**, take the track that climbs away to the L and is signed **GR 201** to Amieva (0.6km; 930m). The track climbs steadily through trees, mostly oak and hazel, with Peña Beza dominating the view ahead. Beech takes over from oak as you gain altitude, then the track doubles back on itself (2.2km; 1130m) and the trees recede, signalling that you are

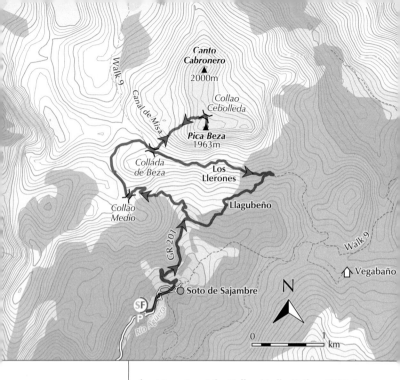

about to arrive at the **Collao Medio** (3.8km; 1380m), an open, grassy col and four large, white stones.

Leave the col and head NW on a narrow, well-used path. This rounds a rocky spur and enters a small valley. Follow the path up the valley as it climbs NE, then E, and finally SE to end at the **Collada de Beza** (5.2km; 1511m).

From the col, climb up NE to the R of a large brown shale scar. Above the scar a narrow path zig-zags up into the **Canal de Misa**, a narrow gash hidden in the apparently impenetrable S wall of Peña Beza. In normal conditions, the scramble up the gash is straightforward, though early in the season this can require care because of old snow. The scrambling comes out at a small col (5.9km; 1705m). ◄

Drop down R from the col to gain the grassy pasture below, and then work quite steeply up below the

Pica Beza is the R-hand of the three rocky summits that can be seen from the Misa col.

Looking up towards the Canal de Misa, the key to access to the Pica Beza summit

W and N walls of Pica Beza to gain a broad, grassy col, the **Collao Cebolleda** (6.4km; 1875m). ▶ Turn S and head up the grassy slope to the foot of the summit rocks. Scramble up these with care and guided by small cairns. The summit of **Pica Beza** (6.6km; 1963m) is reached quite suddenly and offers excellent views in all directions.

Return to the **Collada de Beza** by the ascent route. Once there you can return to Soto by the Collao Medio and the morning's ascent route. However, this is steep, hard on the knees and boring. Instead, leave Collada de Beza (7.9km; 1511m) heading down ESE on narrow animal paths. After 1km the path enters woodland and a chaos of large boulders. Known as **Los Llerones**, this section requires attention as it is easy to get distracted by the surroundings and loose the best path.

The Collao Cebolleda stops you in your tracks because of the views it yields of the Western Massif summits.

Los Llerones is the product of the boulders that have come down from the S walls of Peña Beza. Over time, beech trees have taken root among them and the forest has taken over, although in many places the tree roots have woven themselves so completely into the rock that it is hard to know where stone ends and wood begins.

After leaving Los Llerones the path crosses an open section, re-enters woodland and suddenly comes out at a junction with an old grassy track (9.9km; 1350m). Going L here would take you to Vegabaño; instead turn R and follow the track. This soon narrows to a path but is easily followed as it descends SW to the livestock pens at **Llagubeño** (10.9km; 1240m). From the livestock pens follow a good track to its junction with the morning ascent track (11.7km; 1130m). Continue easily down to **Soto**, the car park (13.9km; 910m) and the end of an excellent walk. ◄

The views down to Soto and beyond to Sajambre are very good over this final section of descent.

Like many small villages around Spain, Soto de Sajambre benefitted from the good fortune of one of its sons. In this case, the benefactor was **Félix de Martino**, an 'Indiano'. The term *Indiano* was used to refer to those who had returned successfully to Spain after emigrating to the Americas during the 19th century. De Martino returned from Mexico at the very beginning of the 20th century and financed the construction of the school, as well as other public amenities such as the road from Oseja and a small hydroelectric plant (La Fábrica de Luz). This began operating in 1921 and provided this remote village with electric lighting. It is worth lingering as you pass through Soto, not only to admire the work of Félix de Martino, but also the local architecture and the carved woodwork of the doors and balconies.

WALK 35
Vega Huerta

Start/Finish	Vegabaño parking space
Distance	16.6km
Ascent/Descent	960m
Grade	Difficult
Time	7–8hr
Terrain	A good path up to the Canal del Perro. Steep in places. Irregular rocky ground along the final section to Vega Huerta.
Map	Editorial Alpina, 1:25,000. Picos de Europa, Macizo Occidental
Access	Drive up through Soto de Sajambre and over the river. Turn R at the highest of the houses and follow a reasonably good jeep track for 7km up to a simple parking space in beech woods just before a cattle grid. Alternatively, follow PR-PNPE 9 to Vegabaño and spend the night at the refuge. There is a lot to recommend this option. Allow 1.5hr for the hut approach.
Route finding	Well signed to the start of the Canal del Perro but requires attention along the Camino del Burro.

Vega Huerta is the alpine meadow at the foot of the immense south face of Peña Santa de Castilla. This walk, the standard approach for those wanting to climb there, gives you access to one of the most beautiful high pastures of the Picos de Europa. The adventure, which takes in rich beech woods, heather-clad middle-mountain slopes, and rocky alpine slabs and screes, can be rounded off with an optional ascent of Los Moledizos (2297m). Doing so turns a great day into an outstanding one.

Cross the cattle grid and follow the track through the woods to the NW edge of Vegabaño, a tree-lined meadow. Follow the track as it skirts round the S edge of the meadow. Where it divides, take the L fork down

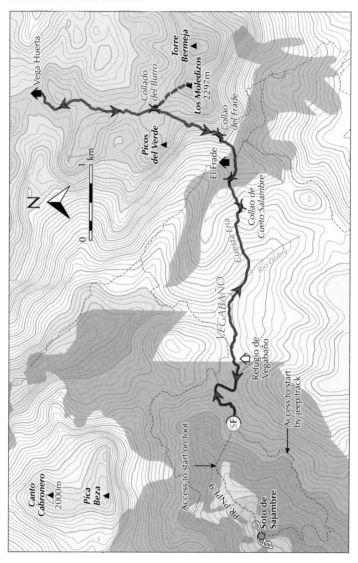

towards the **Vegabaño hut**, but just before the hut (1.3km; 1320m) cut off NNE and go all the way round a fenced field to enter beech woods (1.7km; 1290m).

Follow the path first E then SE to a simple concrete bridge over the **River Dobra** (2.7km; 1300m). Cross the bridge and then follow the well-used path up through the mature beech woods of **Cuesta Fría**.

CUESTA FRÍA

Just after the bridge over the River Dobra an information board explains the significance of Cuesta Fría, which, in 2017 was added to the UNESCO World Heritage list of Ancient and Primeval Beech Forests of the Carpathians and Other Regions of Europe, together with the beech woods in the Canal de Asotín (Walk 29).

Five hundred years ago, Cuesta Fría and other similar areas of the Picos de Europa would have been covered by sessile oak (*Quercus petraea*). Remnants of these ancient trees can be found in in the woods even today, the most obvious being El Roblón, an ancient oak protected by a fence half-way up Cuesta Fría. El Roblón is at least 300 years old, but is now surrounded by beech trees (*Fagus sylvatica*), which are at most, 150 years old.

What is especially interesting is that beech is an exceptionally good 'colonizing' species, and one which from its origins in the Carpathian Mountains 9000 years ago, has spread gradually west, reaching the Picos de Europa relatively recently.

Some distance above El Roblón pass a small spring. The woods die out quite suddenly and you reach the open, grassy **Collao de Cueto Salambre** (3.9km; 1584m). The way ahead lies to the ENE and is totally dominated by the SW walls of Los Moledizos. To the NW you can easily make out the twin summits of Peña Beza and the Canto Cabronero (Walk 34). In the middle distance to the W lie the countless summits of the Cordillera Cantábrica.

Follow the path NE through tall heather and broom to the Collada de Salambre (1693m) above the **shepherd's hut at El Frade**. This is a good place to stop and trace out the route as it works its way round below the walls of Los Moledizos and up into the Canal del Perro.

Continue on up to the **Collao del Frade** (4.7km; 1760m) and excellent views E down into the upper reaches of Valdeón. After a short, steep climb up from the Collao del Frade follow the path as it skirts below the SW walls of Los Moledizos and on up and into the Canal del Perro. In places the path is steep and loose as it zig-zags up in impressive positions. Eventually the angle eases and you come out at the **Collado del Burro** (6.3km; 2132m) and sudden, surprising views of Peña Santa de Castilla to the N.

The route ahead is marked as the Camino del Burro on some maps. Navigation over the next 2km requires you to pay attention even in good weather as the path climbs up and down and swings R and L through a maze of small slabs and tiny hollows (*hoyos*). Just as you begin to run out of patience, swing suddenly NE and drop down into **Vega Huerta** (8.3km; 2030m). Here there is a tiny, unguarded hut, and just below it to the E, a welcome spring.

Peña Santa de Castilla was first climbed in 1892 by the Comte de Saint-Saud, but is best known

among climbers for the routes on its immense south face. The South Face Direct, done in 1947 by three climbers from Madrid, follows an almost vertical line from the foot of the wall directly to the summit. The huge blank walls to the right of the 1947 route were climbed first in the 1980s, while the first ascent of a climb called El Rayu in 2020 brought this great rock face firmly into the modern era.

Arriving at the Collado del Burro and the first glimpse of Peña Santa de Castilla

Return to Vegabaño along the same route. This will not be dull, however, as the sun will have shifted significantly in the sky. Walls that were in shadow in the morning will now be gloriously lit by the afternoon sun.

Once back at the Collado del Burro, it is an easy matter to climb up partially trackless ground SE to the main summit of **Los Moledizos** (2297m). ▶ The summit offers excellent views of the enormous sweep of beech woods

Doing this adds a mere 1.4km, 160m and 1hr to the basic route, so is well worth the effort.

that starts to the E above Fuente Dé, comes around above
Valdeón, and continues unbroken further W along the
slopes of the Cordillera Cantábrica.

WALK 36
Pico Jario

Start/Finish	Vegabaño parking space
Distance	10.9km
Ascent/Descent	750m
Grade	Moderate
Time	5hr
Terrain	Mostly on good paths. Some rougher terrain before the Jario summit.
Map	Editorial Alpina, 1:25,000. Picos de Europa, Macizo Occidental
Access	Drive up through Soto de Sajambre and over the river. Turn R at the highest of the houses and follow a reasonably good jeep track for 7km up to a simple parking space in beech woods just before a cattle grid. Alternatively, follow PR-PNPE 9 to Vegabaño and spend the night at the refuge. Allow 1.5hr for the hut approach on foot. There is a lot to recommend this option, especially if you want to do Walk 35 as well.
Route finding	Waymarked by cairns and signposts over the first half.

The summits that lie outside the main Picos de Europa massifs regularly give
stunning views not just of the Picos themselves, but of the mountains around
the main range as well. Pico Jario is no exception and, combined with the
traverse to the main summit from Peña Blanca, the ascent of Pico Jario gives
a varied day, with hands-on access to some of the complex geology and the
magnificent plant-life of the area.

From the parking area, cross the cattle grid and follow the track through the woods to the NW edge of

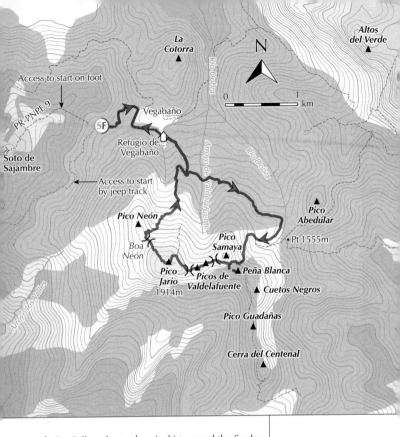

Vegabaño. Follow the track as it skirts round the S edge of the meadow and, when it divides, take the L fork down towards the **Refugio de Vegabaño** (1.4km; 1320m). From immediately behind the hut, cross the wooden bridge over a stream, and walk up to the R of a fenced field to reach a track and hand-painted signs to Puerto de Dobres and Valdeón. After 100m go R at the track junction (more signs) and enter mature beech woods.

The **beech woods** are one of the most attractive features of the Sajambre area. Typical of humid north facing slopes, in Sajambre the beech woods grow on slopes facing in all directions because of the mists that regularly clothe the area's lower reaches.

Almost as soon as you come out of the woods the track swings up and R, but at a rudimentary signpost for Puerto Dobres and Valle Valdeón (2.1km; 1440m), a small path breaks off and climbs up L. Ignoring the track and sign for Pico Jario, follow the small path over quartzite rock in a generally ESE direction, crossing the **Arroyo de Valdelafuente**.

> **Sandstones and quartzites** produce acid soils, as opposed to the alkaline soils that overlie limestones. These changes in acidity are noticeable in the vegetation. Beech trees prefer alkaline soils, while heathers, brooms and gorse thrive on more acidic soils.

Continue to traverse across slopes of bracken, heather and broom. The trees begin to recede and finally you enter a broad, open valley (3.9km; 1540m). This is the upper section of the River Dobra. Peña Blanca (the White Peak), and the Pico Samaya lie to the SW, with the Pico Abedular to the NE. ◄

A few minutes further to the E, the col at Pt 1555 gives excellent views down into Valdeón and is worth a quick visit.

Stay to the R of the Río Dobra, now just a stream, and work up and diagonally R to gain the broad grassy rake that comes down from the Collada de Dobres, the col just to the L(E) of Peña Blanca. Follow the rake up until just below the summit walls of Peña Blanca, then strike off W to gain the Collada Blanca. From there go up SE to the summit of **Peña Blanca** (5.3km; 1805m).

> Although **Peña Blanca** (the White Peak) is off the route, the summit has superb alpine flora because of the alkaline nature of the underlying limestone rocks. It is also a great vantage point, with excellent views of the whole area, and lunch is just as well taken here as on the day's main summit.

When ready, return to the col and work W below the **Samaya** summit. The broom makes progress difficult but the path, though very narrow, is well trodden. From the Colladinos de Samaya (1801m), take the **Picos de Valdelafuente** first on the L and then on the R and so gain the Collado Arroyos (6.1km; 1814m), where the path rises gently over stony ground to come out on a wide grassy slope to the NE of **Pico Jario**. Turn L and head up to the summit, with a short rocky section just before the top (6.6km; 1914m).

The isolated bulk of Peña Beza (Walk 34) and the Canto Cabronero rise to the NW of the Jario. Peña Santa de Castilla (Walk 32) lies to the NNE, the Torre Bermeja (Walk 32) to the ENE, with the Friero group and Collado Jermoso (Walk 29) almost due E. The rest of the horizon from the SE to the NW is a display of over 200km of summits in the Cordillera Cantábrica.

Descend quite comfortably NW to the **Boa Neón** col (7.1km; 1771m). Drop down N here, steeply at first, and follow an intermittent path over mountain pastures in the Upper Valdelafuente valley. ▶ Just as the tree line is

In early summer, the Peña Blanca summit is a feast of flowers

Cattle are completely at home grazing all day in these high summer pastures. This is extensive farming at its very best.

219

reached, a lone cabin off to the L helps you navigate your way into the beech woods (8.3km; 1515m). Enter these to the NE of the cabin. Cairns mark the way through the first trees, and very soon a track is picked up that drops down SE to where you struck off L along the path in the morning. Pick up the morning's track and follow it NW back to **Vegabaño** and then on down to the car park in the woods.

WALK 37
Pueblos de Sajambre

Start/Finish	Park visitor centre, Oseja de Sajambre
Distance	11km
Ascent/Descent	500m
Grade	Moderate
Time	4hr
Terrain	Tracks and good paths with one section of road. Steep from Vistalegre to Ribota.
Map	Editorial Alpina, 1:25,000. Picos de Europa, Macizo Occidental
Access	From Cangas de Onís via the N-625. From Valdeón via the LE-244 and then the N-625 over the Puerto del Pontón.
Route finding	Well signed throughout as PR-PNPE 10

The villages of the Picos de Europa are as much a part of their beauty as the high summits. Starting in Oseja de Sajambre, this walk uses paths, tracks and old drove roads to take you to Soto and Ribota. But the walk is not just traditions and architecture. The scenery walking up to Soto and then down to Ribota adds greatly to the outing. Excellent as a short day, the walk can be done in almost any weather and at any time of the year.

From the National Park visitor centre in **Oseja** (0km; 755m), cross the road and go up the ramp next to the

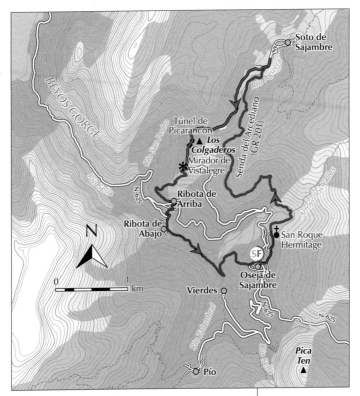

pharmacy. At the very top turn L on a paved road and head NE out of Oseja. On the very outskirts of the town you come to the **San Roque hermitage** (0.6km; 780m) and the chance to look back over the whole of Sajambre. ▸

The walk now enters woodland and follows the **Senda del Arcediano** (GR 201) to Soto de Sajambre. A spring and drinking trough (1.9km; 850m) provide a good excuse to stop and enjoy the views back to Oseja, and these are repeated a little further on as the woodland clears momentarily to the S and W.

One of the national park information boards states that *Sajambre es bosque* (Sajambre is woodland). The section of this walk to Soto de Sajambre is confirmation of the claim, were any needed.

221

Until the construction of the modern road through the Beyos Gorge, goods and merchandise were transported between Cangas de Onís and the north of León along the **Senda del Arcediano**. The Arcediano was the Archdeacon of Villaviciosa, Pedro Díaz de Oseja. In the 17th century he left money in his will for the upkeep of the road. As a recent monument in Soto de Sajambre indicates, drove roads such as this were vital for carrying salt, fish and wood from the coast to the interior, and wine and wheat from Central Spain to the coast.

There are great views of Peña Beza (Walk 34) as you approach Soto.

At a junction in the trail (3.3km; 950m) ignore the option for Vegabaño, and drop down L towards **Soto de Sajambre**, arriving there level with and just below the car park. ◄

EMIGRATION AND THE PICOS DE EUROPA

A park information panel on entering Soto de Sajambre gives information in Spanish about the village. One of the most interesting facts is about **Félix de Martino**, an emigrant who made his fortune in the Americas at the beginning of the 20th century. Despite settling in Mexico, he kept strong ties with his native Soto. He built his house there in 1906, which is known as the *Casa de los Tiros* because of the bullet scars from the Civil War.

De Martino was also behind the building of the spring (*fuente*), the wash-sheds (*lavaderos*) and the school (*escuela*). But his most significant contribution to the village's well-being 100 years ago was the construction of the mini-hydroelectric power station (La Fábrica de Luz), which is tucked away over the river behind the church. Thanks to this forward-thinking piece of engineering, the houses of Soto had electric lighting as early as the 1920s. See Walk 10 for more on emigration.

After visiting Soto de Sajambre, walk SW out of the village along the road. There is normally very little traffic so this is not as grim as it sounds. After passing a small dam (6.3km; 850m) and then a picnic area, follow the road in spectacular positions through the narrow **Túnel de Picarancón** and then on to a lookout point, the **Mirador de Vistalegre** (7.2km; 820m).

The Fábrica de Luz in Soto de Sajambre

Fifty metres on from the lookout, drop down R onto a good but steep path. Descend the open slope with its ample panorama of Sajambre. Enter woodland and come out soon after in **Ribota de Arriba** (8.4km; 600m). Cross the N-625 road diagonally L and go down S on a concreted track, passing among the houses of Ribota de Arriba.

Despite its unlikely position on a steep slope at the entry to the Beyos Gorge, which would have been impenetrable until the 20th century, **Ribota** has been a settlement since at least the 13th century, the date of the now-ruined Ermita (Hermitage) de San Pedro de Orzales. But the numerous 19th-century houses, mostly south facing and with magnificent, glazed balconies, are a clear indication that for a while at least, life in Ribota was not at all bad.

On arrival at the first houses of **Ribota de Abajo** (8.8km; 540m) turn L and go down to the park information panel next to the bridge over the **River Sella**. Go L on a farm track just before the bridge and follow this SE along with the Sella on your R. When the track splits (10.1km; 610m), climb back sharp L and begin the ascent to **Oseja**. This is steep and can be muddy but it leads directly back to the car park for the National Park visitor centre (11km; 755m).

WALK 38

Sajambre es Bosque

Start/Finish	National Park visitor centre, Oseja de Sajambre
Distance	23.9km
Ascent/Descent	1465m
Grade	Very difficult
Time	9–11hr
Terrain	Good trails throughout, except for the descent to Vegabaño.
Map	Adrados Ediciones, 1:50,000. Parque Nacional de los Picos de Europa
Access	From Cangas de Onís along the N-625. From Valdeón along the LE-244 and then the N-625.
Route finding	Straightforward except for the woodland leading to Vegabaño.

The slogan 'Sajambre es bosque' refers to the district's extensive beech woods. This walk takes you through some of the best of these woods, starting and finishing along centuries-old drove roads. In contrast to the woodland, the middle section follows an airy summit ridge that yields boundless views of both the Picos to the north and the Cordillera Cantábrica to the south and west. Soto provides a human touch to this complete, and at times intimate, encounter with the Sajambre sector of the range.

From the National Park visitor centre (0km; 750m) walk up the main road to just before the Mesón del Arcediano, where a side road climbs SE and you pick up signs for the **GR 201**. When you reach a small park and an information board (0.5m; 800m), follow the track through light woodland as it swings first NE and then back towards the south.

When you come out of the woods, an airy section of the track yields an impressive view of the Pica de Ten and the N-625 and takes you to a **lookout point** with an information panel and unfettered views over the vast beech woods of Sajambre (1.9km; 940m). Soon after this, the track enters more woodland and comes to a gate. The GR 201 goes off R here (2.3km; 960m), but ignore this and take the **PR-PNPE 33** for Panderrueda. When the main track seems to climb back L and up (3.48km; 1070m), go straight ahead following the white and yellow PR paint flashes. At a second junction almost immediately afterwards, go right and down.

An airy section of the trail just before the lookout point

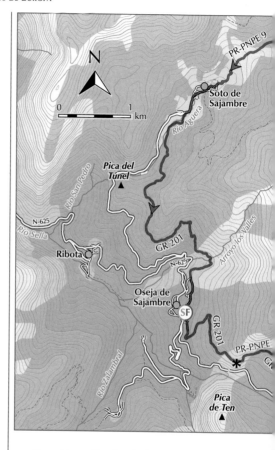

The white walls of rock above and to the L at this point rise up to Peña Blanca (White Peak), which the walk passes later on. The geology throughout this part of the route is fascinating if you are at all geology inclined.

Cross the **Río de los Pontigos** on a small bridge (4.1km; 1090m) and go past a chaos of large conglomerate boulders, and then work steadily but relentlessly up

through magnificent mature beech woods until you reach a new clearing, El Prendao (6.2km; 1335m). ▶

Soon after leaving El Prendao, you come out quite suddenly at the picnic area at **Panderrueda** (7.1km; 1450m) with its excellent views N towards Valdeón and the Central Massif beyond. Leave the picnic area heading N to pick up the obvious track to the **Mirador de Piedrashitas**.

When livestock from Valdeón strayed into this area of Sajambre, it was held captive (prendado) until the corresponding fines were paid.

The Central Massif from the col at Panderrueda

Inaugurated by General Franco in 1967, and very much a statement of its time and the way the dictatorship viewed Spain's natural resources, the **Mirador de Piedrashitas** is one of a number of superb lookout points in and around the Picos De Europa.

A small path leads N away from the back edge of the monument, taking you through the beech woods below the E walls of the **Pico Camborisco**. After crossing a stream, the woods die out and the path crosses the stream for the second time then swings L (sign to Vegabaño) to climb WSW up and parallel to the stream.

The path comes out at the **Collado Viejo** (9.1km; 1630m) and glimpses of the Sajambre district to the W. Turning N here, climb up heather-covered slopes towards the rocky southern edge of the Cerra del Centena. Traverse under this, but not without taking time to marvel at the conglomerate rock and its multi-coloured lichens and rock plants. Once beyond the edge, the route takes you on a delightful dance N between Sajambre on the L and Valdeón to the R. ◀

Peña Santa de Castilla and the Torre Bermeja constantly demand your attention over this section.

The rock type most evident in the Picos de Europa is **Carboniferous mountain limestone**. This solid, pale grey rock makes up most of the three massifs, but is only one of a number of sedimentary and metamorphic rock types visible in the range. Conglomerate and metamorphic rocks are in evidence, for example, to the south of the Sajambre, Valdeón and Liébana valleys. The nature of an area's underlying rock types often surfaces in the names of summits. Quartzite rocks, for example, although almost white when newly exposed, attract dark-coloured lichens. This often gives rise to summits having names like Peñas Negras or Cuetos Negros. Limestones, on the other hand, give rise to names like Peña Blanca (White Peak), which this walk passes right next to.

Just before the **Cuetos Negros** (10.3km; 1715m), descend L a few metres then continue N before rising gently to the **Colladina Dobres** (11.1km; 1747m), with **Peña Blanca** on your L, and a welcoming view down towards the Vegabaño and the woods above Soto de Sajambre.

Descend NE from the col, picking up a grassy rake (probably on old drove road), but when this dies out at a sign for Vegabaño, Vega de Llós and Caldevilla, swing back S and head towards the River Dobra. Follow the vaguest of paths down to and along the L bank of the stream until just W of the Pt 1555 (12.1km; 1540m). Head NNE on a vague path that enters the beech woods and improves as it works its way NW to cross the **Arroyo de Valdelafuente** to reach a junction with a track (14km; 1435m).

Follow the track down through the woods to a clearing, cross a better track, and walk NW on a well-used path, going over a stream and up to the **hut at Vegabaño** (15.1km; 1320m). In terms of navigation, this is the end of the most difficult part of the walk.

A night in Vegabaño has a lot to recommend it. Apart from making the walk less exacting, it gives you the opportunity to enjoy the evening sun on the surrounding summits, notably Peña Beza (Walk 34) and Peña Santa de

Castilla (Walk 35). As a minimum, the hut will serve as a place to take a well-deserved rest and refreshment.

From the hut skirt around the W side of **Vegabaño**, heading for the cabins and information boards on the N side of the meadow. Pick up a good track here, part of the **PR-PNPE 9**, and follow it down through the woods to a point where the path for the PR 9 breaks off sharp R (16.7km; 1250m). Follow the path to where it crosses the **River Agüera** and comes out of the woods (17.5km; 1065m). Descend SW through hay meadows to **Soto de Sajambre** (18.5km; 917m) and another chance to rest and refresh.

Walk down through Soto. Just after the last house on your R there is a park information panel and a path going off R to the car park. Ignore this and continue a few more metres until a track drops down L off the road (19.1km; 900m). This is signed PR-PNPE 10 and **GR 201**, and is the Senda del Arcediano, an ancient drove road that linked Asturias to León. ◄

Follow the trail as its climbs gently parallel to the River Agüera. At a junction with a track coming down from Vegabaño (20.6km; 950m), descend gently S until the track swings E and rewards you with magnificent views of Oseja (21.5km; 890m). ◄

Follow the trail down to the outskirts of **Oseja de Sajambre**, going past the San Roque Hermitage, and yet more outstanding views of the town and its surroundings. Staying above the houses, follow a paved lane until it is possible to turn R and go down a steep path and come out at the pharmacy and the National Park visitor centre (23.9km; 750m).

For more information about the attractive and at the same time intriguing village of Soto de Sajambre, as well as about the Senda del Arcediano, see the comments for Walks 9, 34 and 37.

With or without the overnight stop in Vegabaño, the view of Oseja is a moment to be savoured.

TREKKING

The central section of the Cares gorge (Trek 2 Day 1)

Walkers trekked in the Picos de Europa long before the term came into common use. Nonetheless, recent years have seen a significantly increased interest in trekking, in part as a response to an initiative by the hut wardens from the three massifs. Together they launched Los Anillos de Picos de Europa, three circular treks of varying length and difficulty which take walkers to the most significant places in the range. The shortest of the three *anillos* (rings) is Trek 1 around the Western Massif, but if you want to tackle the two longer options, full details can be found at: http://elanillodepicos.com/home/. However, I didn't want to be restricted to stages that led to huts, and Treks 2 and 3 compliment Trek 1 by covering the Central and Eastern Massifs, respectively. Finally, Trek 4 follows GR 202, the Ruta de la Conquista.

WARNING

I have included overall GPX files for each of the four treks outlined below, but these were generated from digital maps. They are not drawn directly from my own walking, unlike the other GPS tracks in the guide.

TREK 1
Tour of the Western Massif

Start/Finish	Posada de Valdeón
Distance	56.5km
Ascent/Descent	3510m
Grade	Difficult
Time	4 days
Terrain	Tough and trackless over much of Day 2. A long, steep descent on the morning of Day 4.
Map	Editorial Alpina, 1:25,000. Picos de Europa, Macizo Occidental
Access	Start in the main square in Posada de Valdeón, which can be accessed easily by car from anywhere in Valdeón.
Route finding	Mostly straightforward, but trackless over the central section of Day 2

This trek coincides with the Anillo Vindio, the most accessible of the three official Picos treks. The name is a reference to the presence of the Romans in this part of Spain, and to Mons Vindio, the name they gave to mountains in an area that largely coincides with the Picos de Europa.

DAY 1
Posada de Valdeón–Refugio de Vegabaño

Start	Posada de Valdeón
Distance	9.9km
Ascent/Descent	695m/300m
Time	4–5hr

A gentle day to start, mainly on good tracks and paths that take you through superb beech woods.

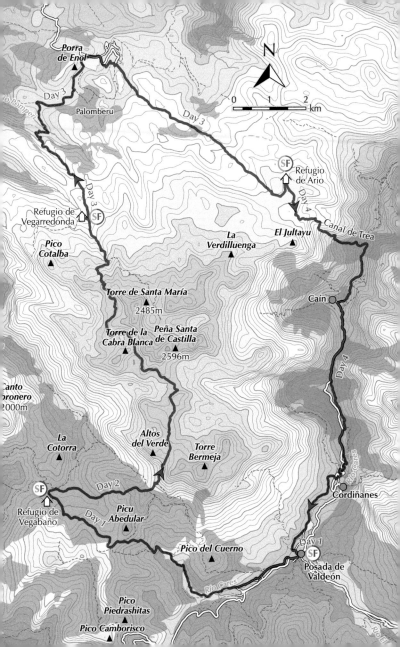

DAY 2
Refugio de Vegabaño–
Refugio de Vegarredonda

Start	Refugio de Vegabaño
Distance	15.2km
Ascent/Descent	1415m/1265m
Time	8–9hr

The toughest day on the trek. From Vega Huerta, the trek skirts around the western edge of the Picos over tough, sometimes trackless and uncomfortable terrain.

DAY 3
Refugio de Vegarredonda–Refugio
de Ario via Los Lagos

Start	Refugio de Vegarredonda
Distance	16.3km
Ascent/Descent	825m/655m
Time	6hr

A gentler day after the rigours of Day 2. Good paths throughout, and with them the chance to take things easy.

DAY 4
Refugio de Ario–
Posada de Valdeón

Start	Refugio de Ario
Distance	15.1km
Ascent/Descent	575m/1290m
Time	6–7hr

The morning will prove hard on the legs for many, with the steep and seemingly endless descent of the Canal de Trea. Caín will feel like paradise in comparison.

TREK 2
Tour of the Central Massif

Start/Finish	Poncebos
Distance	63km
Ascent/Descent	3055m
Grade	Moderate
Time	4 days
Terrain	Good tracks and paths. Very exposed along Cares Gorge and on the descent from Bulnes.
Map	Adrados Ediciones, 1:50,000. Parque Nacional de los Picos de Europa.
Access	By bus, taxi or car from Arenas de Cabrales to Poncebos.
Route finding	Straightforward. Well signed throughout and mostly on waymarked routes.

This is a low-level trek that includes 'must-dos' for the Picos de Europa, such as the Cares Gorge and the village of Bulnes. The trek is within the reach of walkers of all levels, with the first two nights being spent in villages.

DAY 1
Poncebos–Posada de Valdeón

Start	Poncebos
Distance	20.9km
Ascent/Descent	885m/170m
Time	6–7hr

The Cares Gorge, but from Poncebos up to Posada de Valdeón. A good path to Caín and then paths and a short section of road to Posada.

DAY 2
Posada de Valdeón–Espinama

Start	Posada de Valdeón
Distance	15.8km
Ascent/Descent	925m/970m
Time	7–8hr

Good paths and tracks throughout following the PR-PNPE 15, the Senda del Mercadillo, an ancient drove road connecting Valdeón to Camaleño.

DAY 3
Espinama–Refugio de la Terenosa

Start	Espinama
Distance	17.6km
Ascent/Descent	1085m/665m
Time	8–9hr

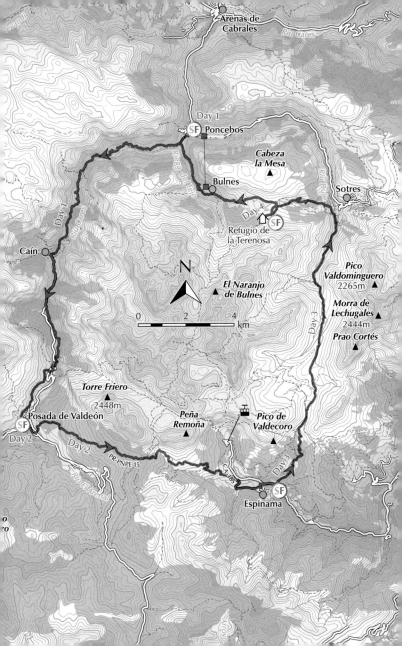

A jeep track connects Espinama with Sotres via the Nevandi and Duje river valleys. Impressive high-mountain scenery throughout, and a night in the tiny La Terenosa refuge.

DAY 4
Refugio de la Terenosa–Poncebos

Start	Refugio de la Terenosa
Distance	8.7km
Ascent/Descent	160m/1250m
Time	3–4hr

An easy day as it is downhill all the way. Great views of El Naranjo de Bulnes to start things off, Bulnes midway, and the exposed path down the Texu Gorge to finish.

TREK 3
Tour of the Eastern Massif

Start	Mogrovejo
Finish	Potes
Distance	41.9km
Ascent	2460m
Descent	2815m
Grade	Moderate
Time	3 days
Terrain	Good tracks and paths. A steep descent on Day 3.
Map	Editorial Alpina, 1:25,000. Picos de Europa, Macizo Central y Oriental
Access	By bus to Camaleño or taxi to Mogrovejo.
Route finding	Straightforward

Time and again walkers ignore the Eastern Massif for the greater draw of the other two. Their mistake. The Eastern

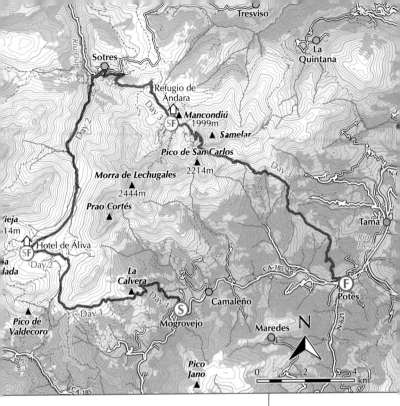

Massif provides some great walking and combines days
in the valleys with a finale in the high mountains.

DAY 1
Mogrovejo–Hotel de Áliva

Start	Mogrovejo
Distance	11.6km
Ascent/Descent	1120m/100m
Time	6–7hr

A fairly gentle start along the N edge of Liébana and then over a little-used pass to reach the Hotel de Áliva and a night amid glorious mountain pastures.

DAY 2
Hotel de Áliva–Refugio de Ándara

Start	Hotel de Áliva
Distance	15.3km
Ascent/Descent	880m/835m
Time	7–8hr

An easy start to the morning following the River Duje, then a long but steady climb up to the hut at Ándara, with Sotres en route for refreshments.

DAY 3
Refugio de Ándara–Potes

Start	Refugio de Ándara
Distance	15km
Ascent/Descent	460m/1880m
Time	5–6hr

A high-mountain day to end with the option of the Samelar or Pico de San Carlos summits before the long descent into Liébana and arrival in the main square of Potes.

TREK 4
Ruta de la Reconquista – GR 202

Start	Covadonga
Finish	Cosgaya
Distance	70.3km
Ascent	4395m
Descent	3945m
Grade	Difficult
Time	4 days
Terrain	Reasonable paths. A hard descent on Day 2.
Map	Editorial Alpina, 1:25,000. Picos de Europa
Access	Bus, taxi or car to Covadonga from Cangas de Onís
Route finding	Mostly straightforward with good waymarking.

The trek coincides with the GR 202 or Ruta de la Reconquista, the national park walk that follows the same route as the Moors who fled south after being defeated at Covadonga. The park description for the GR 202 involves a truly gruelling first day from Covadonga to Poncebos. To avoid this, Day 1 stops at the Vega de Enol refuge, and for the same reason Day 2 breaks at Sotres.

DAY 1
Covadonga–Vega de Enol

Start	Covadonga
Distance	12.5km
Ascent/Descent	1165m/310m
Time	6hr

Uphill all the way, but never dull. Reasonable paths and good waymarking as for GR 202. At the Buferrera car park you need to head W into the Vega de Enol.

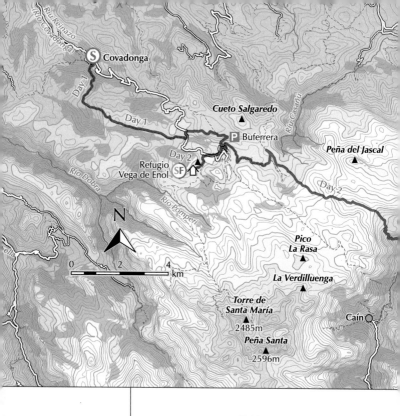

DAY 2

Vega de Enol–Poncebos

Start	Vega de Enol
Distance	21.8km
Ascent/Descent	1020m/1915m
Time	8–10hr

Even if you overnight in the Vega de Enol, this is still a long day, and one that ends with a punishing descent from Vega Maor to the Cares Gorge. Reasonable paths.

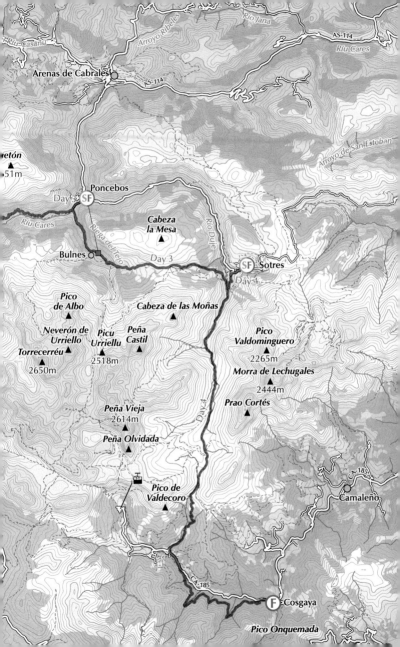

DAY 3
Poncebos–Sotres

Start	Poncebos
Distance	12.2km
Ascent/Descent	1260m/450m
Time	6–7hr

A straightforward day on good paths and tracks, but a lot of uphill, although you could take the funicular to Bulnes could lighten your load.

DAY 4
Sotres–Cosgaya

Start	Sotres
Distance	23.9km
Ascent/Descent	950m/1270m
Time	8–9hr

The easiest day with good tracks throughout. A chance to relax and enjoy the scenery of the Duje valley and Puertos de Áliva. Make sure you book into a good hotel near Cosgaya.

APPENDIX A
Useful contacts and website addresses

Transport

Bus
ALSA
Bus services on the Asturian side of the Picos, including to the Covadonga lakes
www.alsa.com/en/web/bus/home

Autobuses Palmera
www.autobusespalomera.com

Funicular
Bulnes
Rack-and-pinion railway from Poncebos
www.alsa.com/en/web/bus/regional/asturias/bulnes-funicular

Taxi
TaxiturTaxi service from Cangas de Onís and/or Covadonga to the Covadonga lakes www.taxitur.es

Cabrales www.cabrales.es/taxis

Valdeón www.valledevaldeon.es/en

Cable Car
Fuente Dé https://entradas.telefericofuentede.com

Accommodation
www.casamundo.co.uk

www.rentalia.com/holiday-rentals-picos-de-europa

www.valledevaldeon.es/en

Camping Covadonga, Cangas sector
www.camping-covadonga.com

Camping Picos de Europa, Cangas sector
www.picos-europa.com

Camping Naranjo de Bulnes, Cabrales sector
www.campingnaranjodebulnes.com

Camping La Viorna, Liébana sector
www.campinglaviorna.com

Camping La Isla, Liébana sector
www.campinglaislapicosdeeuropa.com

Camping San Pelayo, Liébana sector
www.campingsanpelayo.com

Camping El Redondo, Liébana sector
www.campingfuentede.com

Camping El Cares, Valdeón sector
www.campingelcarespicosdeeuropa.com/en

The National Park
National Park official website, with information about access to the Covadonga lakes, the Cares Gorge and Sotres
www.parquenacionalpicoseuropa.es/english/

La Fonseya Information Centre, Sajambre sector
www.turismocastillayleon.com/en (and search for "La Fonseya Information Center")

English-language introductory leaflet to the Picos de Europa
www.parquenacionalpicoseuropa.es
(go to "visitas" then "folletos", and download the pdf of the leaflet)

Plants, wildlife and traditions
Report in English on lammergeiers in the Picos de Europa
www.eucan.org.uk/docs/201106Sp/
Poppy_Wood.pdf

Centro de Interpretación de la Fauna Glacial de Avín, Asturias
https://www.onis.es/centro-de-interpretacion-de-la-fauna-glacial

Alpine Garden Society Study Tour to the Picos de Europa
www.alpinegardensociety.net/plants/
the-picos-2

An excellent way to gain a deeper understanding of the mountain plants and flowers of the Picos

Fundación Cabrales show cave
www.fundacioncabrales.com/
cueva-exposicion

GPS tracks, walk information and suggestions
GPS tracks for all three Anillos de Picos treks mentioned at the start of the trekking section can be downloaded for free at
www.edicionesdesnivel.com/
tracks-anillo-picos

APPENDIX B
Glossary

Spanish (Castilian/Asturian)	English
aguja	needle
albergue	hostel, usually with shared rooms
arroyo	stream
ayuntamiento	town hall
braña	summer grazing area with shepherds' cabins
cabaña	shepherd's cabin
cabeza/o	secondary summit (mainly in the Cabrales area)
camino	footpath or livestock trail
canal	gully
canalizo	water-worn grooves in limestone slabs or walls
capilla	chapel
carretera	road
collado/a	col
colláu	col (Asturian)
cruce	junction
cuesta	mountain slope or incline
cueto	hill
desfiladero	gorge
fuente	spring
garganta	gorge
hito	cairn
horcada	narrow col or gap
hórreo	grain store built on four legs to keep vermin out
hostal	B&B accommodation
hoyo	natural sinkhole or depression typical of mountain limestone

Spanish (Castilian/Asturian)	English
iglesia	church
invernales	winter quarters and grazing for livestock
jitu	cairn (Asturian)
jou	natural sinkhole or depression typical of mountain limestone (Asturian)
lago	lake or tarn
loma	spur
majada	high-mountain summer grazing area with shepherd's cabins
mirador	viewpoint
monte	mid-level scrub or wooded land
orbayu	a fine, wetting mist common in the north of the Picos (Asturian)
peña	mountain or summit
pensión	very simple B&B accommodation
pico	peak or summit
pista	jeep track
polje	large depression often filled with marshy vegetation
prado	meadow
puertos	high-mountain summer pastures
refugio	climbers' hut/refuge
riega	intermittent stream
río	river
senda	path
sierra	ridge or secondary range
torre	tower
valle	valley
vega	high-mountain pasture for summer grazing

Spanish (Castilian/Asturian)	English
Useful words and phrases in an emergency	
¿Habla inglés?	Do you speak English?
Ha habido un accidente	There has been an accident
¿Por favor, me llama al grupo de rescate?	Would you ring the rescue team, please?
Hay una persona herida	There's one person injured
Hay dos/tres personas heridas	There are two/three people injured
Es un hombre/una mujer	It's a man/woman
No es demasiado grave	It's not too serious
Es un accidente (muy) grave	It's a (very) serious accident
La víctima se encuentra en/ cerca de ...	The victim is at/near ...
Las coordinadas de la víctima son ...	The coordinates for the victim are ...

APPENDIX C
Huts of the Picos de Europa

Hut	Places	Altitude	Open	Web	Email/tel
Western Massif					
Vega de Enol	16	1100m	All year	https://refugiovegadeenol.com/	(+34) 699 488 544
Vegarredonda	63	1410m	May–October	www.vegarredondaremis.com	jmalo@hotmail.es, (+34) 985 922 952, (+34) 626 343 366
Vega de Ario	40	1630m	May–October	www.refugiovegadeario.es	refugiodeario@hotmail.com, (+34) 656 843 095, (+34) 984 092 000
Vegabaño	35	1432m	All year, except January–Easter	www.refugiopicos.com	refugiopicos@gmail.com, (+34) 699 633 244
Central Massif					
Collado Jermoso	24	2046m	May–October	www.colladojermoso.com	refugio@colladojermoso.com, (+34) 636 998 727
Jou de los Cabrones	20	2024m	May–October	http://refugiojoudeloscabrones.com/	No email, (+34) 985 925 200, (+34) 650 780 381
Vega Urriellu	96	1960m	March 15–Dec 15	www.refugiodeurriellu.com	contacto@refugiodeurriellu.com, (+34) 984 090 981, (+34) 650 780 381
La Terenosa	20	1330m	All year if reserved in advance	http://facebook.com/refugioterenosa	No email, (+34) 630 552 016, (+34) 984 090 992. No English spoken.

Hut	Places	Altitude	Open	Web	Email/tel
Cabaña Verónica	8	2325m	Easter–October		No email, (+34) 663 51 64 56
Hotel Áliva	70	1666m	June–October	https://cantur.com/instalaciones/7-hotel-aliva	hotelaliva@cantur.com, (+34) 635 425 228
Eastern Massif					
Casetón de Ándara	20	1725m	June 15–Oct 15	www.casetondeandara.com	No email, (+34) 635 425 228

See also: http://elanillodepicos.com/home/ and https://www.reservarefugios.com/en.

DOWNLOAD THE ROUTES
IN GPX FORMAT

All the routes in this guide are available for download from:

www.cicerone.co.uk/536/GPX

as standard format GPX files. You should be able to load them into most online GPX systems and mobile devices, whether GPS or smartphone. You may need to convert the file into your preferred format using a conversion programme such as gpsvisualizer.com or one of the many other such websites and programmes.

When you follow this link, you will be asked for your email address and where you purchased the guidebook, and have the option to subscribe to the Cicerone e-newsletter.

www.cicerone.co.uk

LISTING OF CICERONE GUIDES

BRITISH ISLES CHALLENGES, COLLECTIONS AND ACTIVITIES

Cycling Land's End to John o' Groats
Great Walks on the England Coast Path
The Big Rounds
The Book of the Bivvy
The Book of the Bothy
The Mountains of England & Wales:
    Vol 1 Wales
    Vol 2 England
The National Trails
Walking the End to End Trail

SHORT WALKS SERIES

Short Walks Hadrian's Wall
Short Walks in Arnside and Silverdale
Short Walks in Nidderdale
Short Walks in the Lake District: Windermere Ambleside and Grasmere
Short Walks in the Surrey Hills
Short Walks on the Malvern Hills

SCOTLAND

Ben Nevis and Glen Coe
Cycle Touring in Northern Scotland
Cycling in the Hebrides
Great Mountain Days in Scotland
Mountain Biking in Southern and Central Scotland
Mountain Biking in West and North West Scotland
Not the West Highland Way
Scotland
Scotland's Mountain Ridges
Scottish Wild Country Backpacking
Skye's Cuillin Ridge Traverse ·
The Borders Abbeys Way
The Great Glen Way
The Great Glen Way Map Booklet
The Hebridean Way
The Hebrides
The Isle of Mull
The Isle of Skye
The Skye Trail
The Southern Upland Way
The Speyside Way Map Booklet
The West Highland Way
The West Highland Way Map Booklet
Walking Ben Lawers, Rannoch and Atholl
Walking in the Cairngorms
Walking in the Pentland Hills
Walking in the Scottish Borders
Walking in the Southern Uplands
Walking in Torridon, Fisherfield, Fannichs and An Teallach

Walking Loch Lomond and the Trossachs
Walking on Arran
Walking on Harris and Lewis
Walking on Jura, Islay and Colonsay
Walking on Rum and the Small Isles
Walking on the Orkney and Shetland Isles
Walking on Uist and Barra
Walking the Cape Wrath Trail
Walking the Corbetts:
    Vol 1 South of the Great Glen
    Vol 2 North of the Great Glen
Walking the Galloway Hills
Walking the John o' Groats Trail
Walking the Munros
    Vol 1 – Southern, Central and Western Highlands
    Vol 2 – Northern Highlands and the Cairngorms
Winter Climbs: Ben Nevis and Glen Coe

NORTHERN ENGLAND ROUTES

Cycling the Reivers Route
Cycling the Way of the Roses
Hadrian's Cycleway
Hadrian's Wall Path
Hadrian's Wall Path Map Booklet
The C2C Cycle Route
The Coast to Coast Cycle Route
The Coast to Coast Walk
The Coast to Coast Walk Map Booklet
The Pennine Way
The Pennine Way Map Booklet
Walking the Dales Way
Walking the Dales Way Map Booklet

NORTH-EAST ENGLAND, YORKSHIRE DALES AND PENNINES

Cycling in the Yorkshire Dales
Great Mountain Days in the Pennines
Mountain Biking in the Yorkshire Dales
St Oswald's Way and St Cuthbert's Way
The Cleveland Way and the Yorkshire Wolds Way
The Cleveland Way Map Booklet
The North York Moors
The Reivers Way
Trail and Fell Running in the Yorkshire Dales
Walking in County Durham
Walking in Northumberland
Walking in the North Pennines

Walking in the Yorkshire Dales: North and East
Walking in the Yorkshire Dales: South and West

NORTH-WEST ENGLAND AND THE ISLE OF MAN

Cycling the Pennine Bridleway
Isle of Man Coastal Path
The Lancashire Cycleway
The Lune Valley and Howgills
Walking in Cumbria's Eden Valley
Walking in Lancashire
Walking in the Forest of Bowland and Pendle
Walking on the Isle of Man
Walking on the West Pennine Moors
Walks in Silverdale and Arnside

LAKE DISTRICT

Bikepacking in the Lake District
Cycling in the Lake District
Great Mountain Days in the Lake District
Joss Naylor's Lakes, Meres and Waters of the Lake District
Lake District Winter Climbs
Lake District: High Level and Fell Walks
Lake District: Low Level and Lake Walks
Mountain Biking in the Lake District
Outdoor Adventures with Children – Lake District
Scrambles in the Lake District – North
Scrambles in the Lake District – South
Trail and Fell Running in the Lake District
Walking The Cumbria Way
Walking the Lake District Fells –
    Borrowdale
    Buttermere
    Coniston
    Keswick
    Langdale
    Mardale and the Far East
    Patterdale
    Wasdale
Walking the Tour of the Lake District

DERBYSHIRE, PEAK DISTRICT AND MIDLANDS

Cycling in the Peak District
Dark Peak Walks
Scrambles in the Dark Peak
Walking in Derbyshire
Walking in the Peak District – White Peak East
Walking in the Peak District – White Peak West

SOUTHERN ENGLAND

20 Classic Sportive Rides
  in South East England
20 Classic Sportive Rides
  in South West England
Cycling in the Cotswolds
Mountain Biking on the
  North Downs
Mountain Biking on the
  South Downs
Suffolk Coast and Heath Walks
The Cotswold Way
The Cotswold Way Map Booklet
The Kennet and Avon Canal
The Lea Valley Walk
The North Downs Way
The North Downs Way Map Booklet
The Peddars Way and Norfolk
  Coast Path
The Pilgrims' Way
The Ridgeway National Trail
The Ridgeway National Trail
  Map Booklet
The South Downs Way
The South Downs Way Map Booklet
The Thames Path
The Thames Path Map Booklet
The Two Moors Way
The Two Moors Way Map Booklet
Walking Hampshire's Test Way
Walking in Cornwall
Walking in Essex
Walking in Kent
Walking in London
Walking in Norfolk
Walking in the Chilterns
Walking in the Cotswolds
Walking in the Isles of Scilly
Walking in the New Forest
Walking in the North Wessex Downs
Walking on Dartmoor
Walking on Guernsey
Walking on Jersey
Walking on the Isle of Wight
Walking the Dartmoor Way
Walking the Jurassic Coast
Walking the South West Coast Path
  and Map Booklets:
    Vol 1: Minehead to St Ives
    Vol 2: St Ives to Plymouth
    Vol 3: Plymouth to Poole
Walks in the South Downs
  National Park

WALES AND WELSH BORDERS

Cycle Touring in Wales
Cycling Lon Las Cymru
Glyndwr's Way
Great Mountain Days in Snowdonia
Hillwalking in Shropshire
Hillwalking in Wales – Vols 1&2
Mountain Walking in Snowdonia
Offa's Dyke Path

Offa's Dyke Path Map Booklet
Ridges of Snowdonia
Scrambles in Snowdonia
Snowdonia: 30 Low-level and Easy
  Walks – North
Snowdonia: 30 Low-level and Easy
  Walks – South
The Cambrian Way
The Pembrokeshire Coast Path
The Pembrokeshire Coast Path
  Map Booklet
The Severn Way
The Snowdonia Way
The Wye Valley Walk
Walking in Carmarthenshire
Walking in Pembrokeshire
Walking in the Brecon Beacons
Walking in the Forest of Dean
Walking in the Wye Valley
Walking on Gower
Walking the Severn Way
Walking the Shropshire Way
Walking the Wales Coast Path

INTERNATIONAL CHALLENGES, COLLECTIONS AND ACTIVITIES

Europe's High Points
Walking the Via Francigena Pilgrim
  Route – Part 1

AFRICA

Kilimanjaro
Walks and Scrambles in the
  Moroccan Anti-Atlas
Walking in the Drakensberg

ALPS CROSS-BORDER ROUTES

100 Hut Walks in the Alps
Alpine Ski Mountaineering
  Vol 1 – Western Alps
  Vol 2 – Central and Eastern Alps
The Karnischer Hohenweg
The Tour of the Bernina
Trail Running – Chamonix and the
  Mont Blanc region
Trekking Chamonix to Zermatt
Trekking in the Alps
Trekking in the Silvretta and
  Ratikon Alps
Trekking Munich to Venice
Trekking the Tour of Mont Blanc
Walking in the Alps

PYRENEES AND FRANCE/SPAIN CROSS-BORDER ROUTES

Shorter Treks in the Pyrenees
The GR10 Trail
The GR11 Trail
The Pyrenean Haute Route
The Pyrenees
Walks and Climbs in the Pyrenees

AUSTRIA

Innsbruck Mountain Adventures
Trekking in Austria's Hohe Tauern
Trekking in Austria's Zillertal Alps
Trekking in the Stubai Alps
Walking in Austria
Walking in the Salzkammergut:
  the Austrian Lake District

EASTERN EUROPE

The Danube Cycleway Vol 2
The Elbe Cycle Route
The High Tatras
The Mountains of Romania
Walking in Bulgaria's National Parks
Walking in Hungary

FRANCE, BELGIUM AND LUXEMBOURG

Camino de Santiago – Via Podiensis
Chamonix Mountain Adventures
Cycle Touring in France
Cycling London to Paris
Cycling the Canal de la Garonne
Cycling the Canal du Midi
Cycling the Route des Grandes Alpes
Mont Blanc Walks
Mountain Adventures in the
  Maurienne
Short Treks on Corsica
The GR5 Trail
The GR5 Trail – Benelux and
  Lorraine
The GR5 Trail – Vosges and Jura
The Grand Traverse of the
  Massif Central
The Moselle Cycle Route
The River Loire Cycle Route
The River Rhone Cycle Route
Trekking in the Vanoise
Trekking the Cathar Way
Trekking the GR20 Corsica
Trekking the Robert Louis
  Stevenson Trail
Via Ferratas of the French Alps
Walking in Provence – East
Walking in Provence – West
Walking in the Ardennes
Walking in the Auvergne
Walking in the Briannonais
Walking in the Dordogne
Walking in the Haute Savoie: North
Walking in the Haute Savoie: South
Walking on Corsica
Walking the Brittany Coast Path

GERMANY

Hiking and Cycling in the
  Black Forest
The Danube Cycleway Vol 1
The Rhine Cycle Route
The Westweg
Walking in the Bavarian Alps